Distinguished Indian Personalities

Vikash Kumar Bhakat

AF529002

SPI PUBLICATIONS

This book has been published with all reasonable efforts taken to make the material error-free after the consent of the author. No part of this book shall be used, reproduced in any manner whatsoever without written permission from the author, except in the case of brief quotations embodied in critical articles and reviews.

The Author of this book is solely responsible and liable for its content including but not limited to the views, representations, descriptions, statements, information, opinions and references ["Content"]. The Content of this book shall not constitute or be construed or deemed to reflect the opinion or expression of the Publisher or Editor. Neither the Publisher nor Editor endorse or approve the Content of this book or guarantee the reliability, accuracy or completeness of the Content published herein and do not make any representations or warranties of any kind, express or implied, including but not limited to the implied warranties of merchantability, fitness for a particular purpose. The Publisher and Editor shall not be liable whatsoever for any errors, omissions, whether such errors or omissions result from negligence, accident, or any other cause or claims for loss or damages of any kind, including without limitation, indirect or consequential loss or damage arising out of use, inability to use, or about the reliability, accuracy or sufficiency of the information contained in this book.

Published by **SPI Publications**, www.spipublications.in
SPI, the **SPI logo**, and **Split Poetry India** are trademarks of **SPI Publications**, or its affiliates.
ISBN-13: 978-81-992622-9-4

First Edition 2025

SPI Publications

Corporate & Editorial Office
117/2, Sector 37, Khandsa Road,
Gurgaon, Haryana 122 001
Phone: +91 98355 52940
Email: contact@spipublications.in
Website: www.spipublications.in

Processed and Printed in India

Acknowledgments

My maternal uncles, Mr. Tapan Kumar Bhakat (Advocate) Mr. Narayan Bhakat (Teacher), Mr. Kishore Kumar Bhakat (Advocate), Mr. Hiranmoy Bhakat (Doctor), Mr. Chandan Kumar Bhakat (Teacher), and Mr. Navin Kumar Bhakat (VLW Officer), are all deserving of my love and gratitude for their support, affection, and guidance throughout my time as a student.

I am also thankful to my late maternal grandparents, grandfather Late Tulsi Bhakat, and my maternal uncles, Late Dilip Kumar Bhakat and Late Prabir Kumar Bhakat, who all had aspirations for my success.

They wanted me to work with pens and papers only so I became a writer.
Heartfelt gratitude to Late Prof Dr PC Bhakat (HOD in Economics in Tata College, Chaibasa) who always inspired and appreciated me for my writing and oratorical prowess.
I am thankful to my uncles Mr Sukumar Bhakat (SPM India Post) and Mr Raju Narayan Bhakat for their love and affection for my education oriented activities.
I shall remain obliged to my uncle Mr Ashok Kumar Bhakat who taught me vocabulary during my initial stage of learning English.
I extend my sincere thanks to my friends Mr Daniel Mbarubukeye
(COUNTRY : RWANDA (Africa)
CITIZEN : RWANDAN
(Education: Masters degree in Education management and administration, *on going* Bachelor degree in Arts and modern languages, specialist in arts and publishing) and Mr Charles Ndayizeye (Graduation in English Language & Literature) from Bujumbura, Burundi (Africa) both the foreign friends communicate with me through WhatsApp chatting, voice and video calling and facebook as well. They like my poems and articles so much and praise me for writing and communication skills in English. Mr Charles has even read and wrote a review on my novel Unforgettable Memories.
I especially thank the critics for their criticism which has always been an energy booster for me to be able to write books. I have written many books. Most of them are available globally. I have been co - author of many books.

Preface

Biographies Of 21 Great Indians written by Vikash Kumar Bhakat.
This book contains biographies of 21 Great Indians, whose stories inspire many people to accomplish great things in their lives. All 21 outstanding Indians featured here had a significant effect across the globe. They were really gems of our country. Their ideologies inspire us a lot. Without a question, they accomplished a great deal in their sector.

Those who want to do something different in their life can benefit from this book.

About The Author

Vikash Kumar Bhakat is a poet, writer, author, novelist, teacher and social & educational entrepreneur from Shankarda village near Jamshedpur, Jharkhand.
The author is the Author/President of Vikash Educational & Charitable Trust and the Founder Director of Pioneer English School, Janamdih under Potka block in Jharkhand.
He had been living in Mumbai for more than a half decade.
He came back from Mumbai with an intention to impart English education in remote areas.
He imparts free English education to the underprivileged students.
He knows about the significance of English education and its needs in rural areas.
He has obtained his basic education living at his maternal uncle's home at Upperbandha (2)village .
He has secured a first class position in BA English Language & Literature.
Whatever he is today due to his maternal grandparents, grandparents and parents.
Total credit goes to them and this is even dedicated to them.
Being a social and educational entrepreneur he is always engaged in social and educational activities.
He helped so many needy people during the lockdown including stranded migrant labourers with the assistance of MPs, MLAs, Bureaucrats, Social Activists etc. from various parts of the country.
He got seven stranded migrant workers rescued by the DCP Mr Karun Uddavrao of South Madurai. By the request of the author three stranded migrant workers were rescued by the PA of the honorable MLA Mr Jignesh Mevani from Morbi,Gujarat.
The author has been writing articles on several issues.
He is a bilingual writer who writes in English as well as in Hindi.

Vikash Kumar Bhakat
At + Po - Shankarda
Via - Sundernagar
Dist - East Singhbhum (Jharkhand)
PIN - 832107
Email ID vikashkumarbhakat@gmail.com
7779868295
8340583812

1.Ramkrishna Paramhans

He had a longing to see God since childhood, having grown up in a religious and devotional milieu in a Bengal hamlet. Human worshipper Ramakrishna Paramhans has held the belief that God is visible since he was a little boy. To reach God, he practiced strict sadhana and dedication. He concluded that all world religions are true and that there is no distinction between them as a result of sadhana. They just use various methods to get to God. Gadhdhar got a boil between his eyebrows when he was seven years old. After rendering him unconscious, the doctor explained that the boil would need to be excised. The youngster stated that there was no need to render him unconscious; simply cut it, and I would not move.

Gadhdhar lost his father when he was just seven years old. Under such unfavorable conditions, it became challenging to support the whole family. Despite facing financial challenges, Gadhdhar's bravery remained unwavering. Ramkumar Chattopadhyay, his older brother, was the head of a Calcutta (Kolkata) school. He accompanied Gadhdhar to Kolkata. A few days later, he was sent to worship in the temple of Dakshineshwar, dedicated to Rani Rashmoni. He submitted himself at Maa Mahakali's feet. He would meditate for hours and would be so engrossed in the devotion of the mother that people would consider him mad. He would concentrate for hours, yearning for the mother's darshan. When his restlessness reached a climax one night at midnight, Jagadamba arrived and granted his request. Gadhdhar is now known as Paramhansa Ramakrishna Thakur. An elderly sanyasini made Paramhansa ji undertake several tantric sadhnas during this period. Apart from her, a Vedanti Mahatma named Totapuri also had a great influence on Paramhans Ji. He taught Paramhans Ji the Advaita principle. His significance stems from his renunciation, detachment, and unwavering commitment, as well as the sermons he delivered that helped thousands of people and whose ideas impacted academics like Keshav Chandra Sen, president of the Brahmo Samaj. An atheist and rational young man like Narendra was changed by this influence and spiritual force into Swami Vivekananda, a fervent believer and ambassador of India's glory. He preached in an emotive and straightforward manner. He would convey the whole message in a small example. He consistently advocated for social change by love, compassion, and service. He declared that he was totally devoted to Indian culture and philosophy. He believed in the truth in religions.

Ramakrishna Ji considered idol worship as a means of achieving God, although he focused more on self-purification than on symbols and rituals. In Bengal, child marriage is a common practice. Gadhdhar was also married in childhood. When his young wife Sharadamani came to Dakshineshwar, Gadhdhar had already become Vitrag Paramhansa. Mother Sharadamani says - Is it not my good fortune that I get to see Thakur once? Paramhansa Ji used to say, "The mother who cares for the world and is enthroned on the Peeth in the temple is the same." These were his thoughts on his wife Maa Sharadamani. In the year 1859, he married Sharada Devi. Sharada Devi was 14 years old when she married Ramakrishna, who was 23. Sharada Devi went to the Dakshinor temple to meet Ramakrishna when she was 18 years old. When Sharada Devi arrived at Ramakrishna Paramhansa, she had begun living as an ascetic. Ramakrishna revered his wife as Maa Jagdamba. Their relationship remained solely spiritual. Sri

Ramakrishna educated Sharada Devi in all aspects of life, including household chores and Brahma Gyan. Like Ramakrishna, Sharada Devi achieved the pinnacle of spirituality. Devotees

now refer to Sharada Devi as Maa Sharada. In Ramakrishna's view, the one whose discretion and detachment remain intact even while living near his wife is considered to be truly established in Brahma. The one who sees both man and woman as equal souls and behaves accordingly can be considered a true Brahma Gyani.

2. Swami Vivekananda

Born on January 12, 1863, and passed away on July 4, 1902

Basic principles of Swami Vivekananda's educational philosophy

The goal of education should be to help children grow physically, mentally, and spiritually.
Education should be designed to help children develop their character, their intelligence, and their ability to support themselves.
Both boys and girls deserve equal schooling.
Religious education should be provided by behavior and sanskars rather than through literature.
Both worldly and spiritual issues should be included in the curriculum.
Education can be obtained in the Guru's residence.
The teacher-student relationship should be as intimate as possible.
The entire population should be encouraged to learn more.
To advance the nation's economy, plans for technical education should be put in place.
Family education should be the first step in humanitarian and national education.

Swami Vivekananda was a well-known and significant Vedic spiritual teacher. Narendra Nath Dutt was his true name. At the 1893 World Religion Conference in Chicago, USA, he spoke for India on behalf of Sanatan Dharma. Swami Vivekananda's talks helped spread India's spiritual Vedanta philosophy to every country in America and Europe. He started the Ramakrishna Mission, which is still active today. He was an excellent disciple of Ramakrishna Paramahamsa. He is most known for beginning his remarks with, "My American brothers and sisters." The first phrase of his speech captivated everyone's hearts. Vivekananda was born into an affluent Bengali family in Calcutta and was drawn to spiritualism. He was highly impacted by his teacher, Ramakrishna Dev, who taught him that all living creatures are incarnations of God himself, and hence God might be served by helping people. Following Ramakrishna's death, Vivekananda traveled extensively throughout the Indian subcontinent, gaining firsthand information of the realities in British India. Later, he traveled to the United States to represent India in the 1893 Parliament of World Religions. Vivekananda taught the concepts of Hindu philosophy in the United States, England, and Europe, giving hundreds of public and private talks. In India, Vivekananda is revered as a patriotic saint, and his birthday is observed as National Youth Day.

Early life

Swami Vivekananda was born into a Kayastha household in Calcutta. His childhood name was Narendranath Dutta. Father Vishwanath Dutta was a well-known lawyer in Calcutta High Court. Durgacharan Dutta, Narendra's grandfather, was a scholar of Sanskrit and Persian. He left his family at the age of 25 to become a monk. His mother, Bhuvaneshwari Devi, held religious sentiments. She spent most of her time worshiping Lord Shiva. Narendra's father and mother's religious, progressive, and rational beliefs influenced his thinking and demeanor. Narendra was both bright and naughty when he was a toddler. He enjoyed playing pranks on his classmates and his professors whenever he had the opportunity. Every day, there was a regular worship service in his home. Mother Bhuvaneshwari Devi, who was devout by nature, loved to hear the Puranic, Ramayana, Mahabharata, and other legends. They used to host storytellers on a regular basis. Kirtans and Bhajans were also routinely held. As a result of the family's religious and spiritual atmosphere, Narendra was instilled with religious and spiritual ideals from an early age. The desire to understand and achieve God began to emerge in the child's mind from an early age as a result of the religious environment and the ideals of the parents. Sometimes, in his curiosity about God, he would pose questions that even his parents and the storyteller Panditji would find perplexing.

Education

At the age of eight, Narendranath enrolled at the Metropolitan Institute of Ishwar Chandra Vidyasagar in 1871. In 1877, his family relocated to Raipur. Following his family's return to Calcutta in 1879, he was the sole student to earn first division in the Presidency College admission test. He studied extensively on philosophy, theology, history, social sciences, art, and literature. He had a keen interest in many Hindu scriptures including the Vedas, Upanishads, Bhagavad Gita, Ramayana, Mahabharata and Puranas. Narendra was trained in Indian classical music, and regularly participated in physical exercises and sports. Narendra studied Western logic, Western philosophy and European history at the General Assembly's Institution (now the Scottish Church College). He passed the Fine Arts examination in 1881, and completed his Bachelor of Arts degree in 1884. Narendra studied the works of David Hume, Immanuel Kant, Johann Gottlieb Fichte, Baruch Spinoza, Georg W. H. Hegel, Arthur Schopenhauer, Auguste Comte, John Stuart Mill and Charles Darwin. He translated Spencer's book Education (1860) into Bengali. He was fascinated by Herbert Spencer's theory of evolution. Along with studying Western philosophers, he also learned Sanskrit texts and Bengali literature. William Hastie (Principal of Mahasabha Institution) wrote, "Narendra is really a genius. I have traveled extensively and in large areas but have not seen a single child with talent like him anywhere, not even among the philosophy students of German universities." Many times he has also been called Shrutidhar (a person with a prodigious memory).

Travels

At the age of 25, Narendra wore saffron clothes. Thereafter, he travelled all over India on foot. In 1893, the World Religious Council was being held in Chicago (America). Swami Vivekananda reached there as India's representative. At that time, the people of Europe and America looked down upon the subjugated Indians. People there tried very hard to ensure that Swami Vivekananda did not get time to speak in the Parliament of Religions. But due to the efforts of an American professor, he got some time. All the scholars were astonished to hear his views in that council. Then he was warmly welcomed in America. A large community of his devotees was formed there. He stayed in America for three years and provided the people there with the wonderful light of Indian philosophy. Looking at his oratory style and knowledge, the media there named him Cyclonic Hindu. "Without spiritual knowledge and Indian philosophy, the world will become orphan", this was Swami Vivekananda's firm belief. He established many branches of Ramakrishna Mission in America. Many American scholars became his disciples. He always called himself a 'servant of the poor'. He always tried to make India's glory shine in foreign countries.

Contribution and importance of Vivekananda

The work done by Swami Vivekananda in his short life of 49 years will continue to guide generations for centuries to come. At the age of 30, Swami Vivekananda represented Hinduism in the World Religion Conference in Chicago, America and gave it universal recognition. Gurudev Rabindranath Tagore once said - "If you want to know India, then read Vivekananda. You will find everything positive in him, nothing negative." Romain Rolland said about him - "It is impossible to even imagine him being second, wherever he went, he was always the first. Everyone saw their leader in him. He was God's representative and his specialty was to gain dominance over everyone. Once in the Himalayan region, an unknown traveler stopped in his tracks after seeing him and shouted in surprise - 'Shiva!' It was as if the person's idol had written his name on his forehead." He was not only a saint but also a great patriot, speaker, thinker, writer and lover of humanity. After returning from America, he had appealed to the countrymen saying- "New India should come out from the cobbler's shop, the blacksmith's furnace, the factory, the market, the bazaar; come out from the bushes, jungles, hills and mountains." And the people responded to Swamiji's call. They came out proudly. The public support that Gandhiji got in the freedom struggle was the result of Vivekananda's call. Thus he became a major source of inspiration for the Indian freedom struggle. He believed that sacred India is the holy land of religion and philosophy. It is here that great Mahatmas and sages were born, this is the land of renunciation and sacrifice and here - only here - from ancient times till today the door to the highest ideal of life and liberation is open for man. His sayings- "Arise, awake, awaken others by awakening yourself. Make your human life successful and do not stop till the goal is achieved." In the last years of the nineteenth century, Vivekananda wanted to liberate the country through armed or violent revolution. But he soon became convinced that the circumstances were not ripe for those intentions. Only after this, Vivekananda followed the policy of 'Ekala Chalo' and explored India and the world as a Parivrajak. He had said that I need many young sanyasis who spread in the villages of India and devote themselves to the service of the countrymen. This dream of his was not fulfilled. Vivekananda was strongly against priestism, religious pomp, dogmatism and orthodoxy. He did spiritual contemplation by keeping religion at the center of service to mankind. His Hindu religion was not strange, slimy and airy. He had given this rebellious statement that the thirty three crore hungry, poor and malnourished people of this country should be installed in temples like gods and goddesses and the idols of gods and goddesses should be removed from the temples.

This timeless call of his raises a big question mark at the end of the first decade of the twenty first century. On hearing his call, the entire priestly class was terrified. Today, not only any other saint, but even the government machinery cannot take the risk of removing the idol of any illegal temple. The underlying theme of Vivekananda's life was that he was convinced that if there is any country on the lap of earth which has made honest efforts for the betterment of man in every way, then it is India. He also ridiculed priestism, Brahmanism, religious rituals and customs and also fought against such anomalies in almost aggressive language. In his view, the essence of the thoughts of the best thinkers of Hinduism is still a matter of envy for the whole world. Swamiji had indicated that there is material prosperity in foreign countries and India needs it too but we should not become beggars. We have much more than we can give to the West and the West desperately needs it. This was not Swami Vivekananda's arrogance or boastfulness about his country's heritage. This was a neutral, objective and value-based criticism of Indian civilization and culture by a Vedantic monk. The history of the twentieth century later endorsed it.

Death

Vivekananda is famous all over the world for his energetic and pithy lectures. On the last day of his life, he interpreted Shukla Yajurveda and said, "One more Vivekananda is needed to understand what this Vivekananda has done till now." According to his disciples, even on the last day of his life, 4 July 1902, he did not change his daily routine of meditation and meditated for two to three hours in the morning and in the meditative state itself, he pierced his Brahmarandhra and attained Mahasamadhi. He was cremated on a sandalwood pyre on the banks of the Ganga in Belur. On the other side of this Ganga bank, his Guru Ramakrishna Paramhansa was cremated sixteen years ago. His disciples and followers built a temple there in his memory and established more than 130 centers to propagate the messages of Vivekananda and his Guru Ramakrishna all over the world.

Vivekananda's philosophy of education

Swami Vivekananda was against the English education system propounded by Macaulay and prevalent at that time, because the aim of this education was only to increase the number of clerks. He wanted such an education which could lead to the all-round development of the child. The aim of the child's education is to make him self-reliant and stand on his own feet. Swami Vivekananda has called the prevalent education as 'negative education' and said that you consider a person educated who has passed some examinations and who can give good speeches, but the reality is that what is the benefit of such education which does not prepare the common people for the struggle of life, which does not build character, which does not develop the spirit of social service and which cannot create courage like a lion. Therefore, Swamiji was not in favor of theoretical education, he considered practical education useful for a person. It is the education of a person that prepares him for the future, so it is necessary to have those elements in education which are important for his future. In the words of Swami Vivekananda, you will have to be practical in all areas of work. Piles of principles have destroyed the entire country. Swamiji wants to prepare people for both worldly and spiritual life through education. From a worldly point of view, he has said about education that 'we need such education which builds character, increases mental strength, develops intellect and makes a person self-reliant.' From a spiritual point of view, he has said that 'education is the expression of man's inherent perfection.'

Important Dates

12 January 1863 -- Born in Calcutta

1879 -- Admission to Presidency College, Calcutta

1880 -- Admission to General Assembly Institution

November 1881 -- First meeting with Ramakrishna Paramahamsa

1882-86 -- Associated with Ramakrishna Paramahamsa

1884 -- Passed graduation examination; Death of father
1885 -- Ramakrishna Paramahamsa's last illness
16 August 1886 -- Ramakrishna Paramahamsa's death
1886 -- Establishment of Varahnagar Math
January 1887 -- Formal vow of sannyasa at Varahnagar Math
1890-93 -- Tour of India as a Parivrajak
25 December 1892 -- At Kanyakumari
13 February 1893 -- First public lecture at Secunderabad
31 May 1893 -- Left for America from Mumbai
25 July 1893 -- Reached Vancouver, Canada
30 July 1893 -- Arrived in Chicago
August 1893 -- Meeting with Prof. John Wright of Harvard University
11 September 1893 -- First lecture at the World's Religion Conference, Chicago
27 September 1893 -- Last lecture at the World's Religion Conference, Chicago
16 May 1894 -- Speech at Harvard University
November 1894 -- Vedanta Samiti established in New York
January 1895 -- Religious classes started in New York
August 1895 -- In Paris
October 1895 -- Lectures in London
6 December 1895 -- Back to New York
22-25 March 1896 -- Again to London
May-July 1896 -- Lectures at Harvard University
15 April 1896 -- Back to London
May-July 1896 -- Religious classes in London
28 May 1896 -- Meeting with Max Muller at Oxford
30 December 1896 -- Leaves Nepal for India
15 January 1897 -- Arrives in Colombo, Sri Lanka
January 1897 -- Warm welcome and speech at Ramanathapuram (Rameswaram)
6-15 February 1897 -- In Madras
19 February 1897 -- Arrives in Calcutta
1 May 1897 -- Establishment of Ramakrishna Mission
May-December 1897 -- Journey to North India

January 1898 -- Return to Calcutta
19 March 1899 -- Establishment of Advaita Ashram in Mayavati
20 June 1899 -- Second trip to Western countries
31 July 1899 -- Arrival in New York
22 February 1900 -- Establishment of Vedanta Samiti in San Francisco
June 1900 -- Last class in New York
26 July 1900 -- Departure to Europe
24 October 1900 -- Journey to Vienna, Hungary, Constantinople, Greece, Egypt etc.
26 November 1900 -- Departure to India
9 December 1900 -- Arrival at Belur Math
10 January 1901 -- Journey to Mayavati
March-May 1901 -- Pilgrimage to East Bengal and Assam
January-February 1902 -- Journey to Bodh Gaya and Varanasi
March 1902 -- At Belur Math Return
4 July 1902 -- Mahasamadhi

3. Mahatma Gandhi

Birth

2 October 1869

Death

30 January 1948

Slogan

Do or die.

I am prepared to die, but there is no cause for which I am prepared to kill.

You will never know who is important to you until you actually lose them.

When you are faced with an opponent, win him by love, win him by non-violence.

Quit India

Introduction

Mahatma Gandhi is considered the leader of the Indian National Movement against British rule and the 'Father of the Nation'. His full name was Mohandas Karamchand Gandhi. He gained international fame for his principle of non-violent protest to achieve political and social progress. Mohandas Karamchand Gandhi was a prominent political and spiritual leader of India and the Indian Independence Movement. He had an unbreakable relationship with 'Sabarmati Ashram'. Mahatma Gandhi remained associated with this ashram throughout his life, which is why he also got the title of 'Saint of Sabarmati'.

Mahatma Gandhi was born on 2 October 1869 at a place called Porbandar in Gujarat. His parents were staunch Hindus. His father's name was Karamchand Gandhi. Mohandas's mother's name was Putlibai who was the fourth wife of Karamchand Gandhi. Mohandas was the last child of his father's fourth wife. His father Karamchand (Kaba Gandhi) was first the Diwan of Porbandar, the capital of a small princely state in the Gujarat state of western India under British rule, and later he was the Diwan in Rajkot (Kathiawar) and Wankaner respectively. Karamchand Gandhi did not receive much formal education, but he was a skilled administrator and knew how to find his way among eccentric princes, their unhappy subjects and the staunch British political officials in power.

In 1887, Mohandas somehow passed the matriculation examination of Bombay University and took admission in Samaldas College in Bhavnagar. Due to the sudden switch from Gujarati to English language, he started having some difficulty in understanding the lectures. Meanwhile, there was a discussion going on in his family about his future. If the decision was left to him, he would have wanted to become a doctor. But apart from the prejudice against dissection in the Vaishnav family, it was also clear that if he had to follow the family tradition of getting a high position in a royal family of Gujarat, he would have to become a barrister. This meant a trip to England and Gandhi, who was not very fond of Samaldas College, gladly accepted this proposal. In his young mind, England was the image of 'the land of philosophers and poets, the center of the whole civilization'. In September 1888, he boarded a ship. 10 days after reaching there, he got admission in 'Inner Temple', one of the four law colleges in London.

At the Durban court, the European magistrate asked him to remove his turban; he refused and walked out of the court. A few days later, while travelling to Pretoria, he was thrown out of a first class railway compartment and spent the night shivering at the station. On the next leg of the journey he was beaten up by a horse-drawn carriage driver for refusing to give way to a European passenger on the footboard, and finally barred from entering hotels reserved for 'Europeans only'. These humiliations were part of daily life for Indian traders and workers in Natal. What was new was not Gandhi's experience but his reaction. Hitherto he had been averse to dogmatism and extremism, but when he had to undergo unexpected humiliations, something changed in him.

In 1906 the Transvaal government issued a particularly humiliating ordinance for the registration of the Indian population of South Africa. Indians held a protest meeting in Johannesburg in September 1906 under Gandhi's leadership and pledged to violate the ordinance and suffer the resulting punishment. Thus was born satyagraha, a new technique of suffering rather than inflicting pain, of neutral resistance and of fighting without violence.

Gandhi's religious quest began in his childhood under the influence of his mother, his home in Porbandar and Rajkot. But it received a major boost on his arrival in South Africa. He was fascinated by Tolstoy's writings on Christianity. He studied translations of the Quran and delved into Hindu scriptures and philosophy. Through the study of relative karma, conversations with scholars and personal reading of theological works, he came to the conclusion that all religions are true and yet each is imperfect because they have sometimes been interpreted with a low mind and narrow mind and often misinterpreted. The Bhagavad Gita, which Gandhi first studied in England, became his 'spiritual dictionary' and probably had the greatest influence on his life. Two Sanskrit words mentioned in the Gita attracted him the most. One was 'aparigraha' (renunciation), which means that a man should give up material things that hinder his spiritual life and he should be free from the bondage of wealth and property. The other word is 'samabhaav' (equanimity of mind), which taught him to remain steadfast in sorrow or happiness, victory or defeat, and to work without hope of success or fear of failure.

4. Subhash Chandra Bose

Birth : 23 January 1897

Death : 18 August 1945

Slogan : Give me blood, I will give you freedom

Netaji Subhash Chandra Bose was born on 23 January 1897 in a prosperous Bengali family of Cuttack in Orissa. Bose's father's name was 'Jankinath Bose' and mother's name was 'Prabhavati'. Jankinath Bose was a famous lawyer of Cuttack city. Prabhavati and Jankinath Bose had a total of 14 children, including 6 daughters and 8 sons. Subhash Chandra was their ninth child and fifth son. Out of all his brothers, Subhash was most attached to Sharadchandra. Netaji did his early education at Ravenshaw Collegiate School in Cuttack. Thereafter, he was educated at Presidency College and Scottish Church College in Calcutta, and later his parents sent Bose to Cambridge University in England to prepare for the Indian Administrative Service (Indian Civil Service). During the British rule, it was very difficult for Indians to join the civil service, but he secured fourth position in the civil service examination. In 1921, on receiving news of increasing political activities in India, Bose withdrew his candidature and returned to India soon. After leaving the civil service, he joined the Indian National Congress. Subhash Chandra Bose did not agree with Mahatma Gandhi's ideas of non-violence. In fact, Mahatma Gandhi led the liberal party, while Subhash Chandra Bose was a favourite of the zealous revolutionary party. Mahatma Gandhi and Subhash Chandra Bose had different ideas, but they knew very well that Mahatma Gandhi and they had the same goal, i.e. freedom of the country. Netaji was the first to address Gandhiji as the Father of the Nation.

After being elected as the President of the Indian National Congress in 1938, he formed the National Planning Commission. This policy was not in accordance with Gandhian economic ideas. In 1939, Bose again emerged victorious by defeating a Gandhian opponent. Gandhi took it as his defeat. On his election as the President, Gandhiji said that Bose's victory is my defeat and it seemed that he would resign from the Congress Working Committee. Due to Gandhiji's opposition, this 'rebel president' felt the need to resign. Seeing Gandhi's continuous opposition, he himself left the Congress. Meanwhile, the Second World War broke out. Bose believed that independence could be achieved by joining hands with the enemies of the British. Seeing his views, the British government detained him in Kolkata but he escaped from there with the help of his nephew Shishir Kumar Bose. He reached Germany via Afghanistan and the Soviet Union.

Before entering active politics, Netaji traveled all over the world. He stayed in Europe from 1933 to 1936. This was the era of Hitler's Nazism and Mussolini's Fascism in Europe. The target of Nazism and Fascism was England, which had imposed one-sided agreements on Germany after the First World War. They wanted to take revenge from England. India was also under British occupation and in the fight against England, Netaji saw future friends in Hitler and Mussolini.

The enemy's enemy is a friend. He believed that to achieve independence, along with political activities, diplomatic and military cooperation is also needed.

Subhash Chandra Bose married his secretary and Austrian girl Emily in 1937. They both had a daughter named Anita who currently lives with her family in Germany. Netaji met Hitler. He did many things for the British rule and the independence of the country. He left Germany in 1943. From there he reached Japan. From Japan he reached Singapore. Where he took command of the Azad Hind Fauj established by Captain Mohan Singh. At that time Ras Bihari Bose was the leader of Azad Hind Fauj. He reorganized Azad Hind Fauj. Rani Jhansi Regiment was also formed for women, whose captain Lakshmi Sahgal became.

Subhash Chandra, famous as 'Netaji', established 'Azad Hind Government' on 21 October 1943 with the aim of making India independent through a strong revolution and formed 'Azad Hind Fauj'. The symbol of this organization was a flag with a picture of a roaring tiger. Netaji reached Burma with his Azad Hind Fauj on 4 July 1944. It was here that he gave his famous slogan, "Tum mujhe khoon do, main tumhe azadi dunga". It is said that Netaji died in an air crash near Taiwan on 18 August 1945 while going to Tokyo (Japan), but his body could not be found. Today we will discuss the reasons for Netaji's death.

5. Chandrashekhar Azad

Birth : 23 July, 1906

Death : 27 February, 1931

Slogan

We will face the enemy's bullets, we are free and will remain free

Pandit Chandrashekhar Azad was born in a tribal village Bhavra on 23 July, 1906. His father Pandit Sitaram Tiwari was a resident of Badar village in Unnao district of Uttar Pradesh. Due to severe famine, he took the help of a relative and settled in Bhavra village of 'Alirajpur Riyasat'. At present Bhavra is a village in Jhabua district of Madhya Pradesh. When Chandrashekhar grew up, he left his parents and ran away and reached Banaras. His uncle Pandit Shivvinayak Mishra lived in Banaras. He took some help from him and also made some arrangements on his own and got admitted in 'Sanskrit Vidyapeeth' and started studying Sanskrit. In those days, there was a wave of non-cooperation movement in Banaras. People used to sit in dharna by lying down in front of shops to ensure that foreign goods were not sold. The Jallianwala Bagh massacre of 1919 deeply saddened him. Half-naked tribal children of a tribal village Bhavra were celebrating Diwali together. Some children had sparklers, some had firecrackers and some had Mehtab matchboxes. Child Chandrashekhar had none of these. He was standing and watching his friends celebrating. The child who had Mehtab matchbox would take out a matchstick from it and holding its tip, he would rub it with the matchbox with fear and when coloured light would come out, he would throw the matchstick on the ground out of fear.

Child Chandrashekhar could not tolerate this, he said- "You cannot light even one matchstick and hold it in your hand out of fear. I can light all the matches together and hold them in my hand." The boy who had Mehtab's matchbox gave it to Chandrashekhar and said, "Do whatever you have said and then I will know." The boy Chandrashekhar took out all the matchsticks and held them in his hand. Those sticks were placed upside down, that is, some of the matches had their grease on the palm of Chandrashekhar. He rubbed the bundle of matches with the matchbox. All the matches lit up with a bang. The matches whose grease was on the palm of Chandrashekhar also started burning and burning his palm. Despite the unbearable burning sensation, Chandrashekhar did not leave the matches until their colourful light ended. When he threw the matches away, he said to his friends, "Look, I did not leave the matches even after my palm was burnt." His friends saw that Chandrashekhar's palm was burnt a lot and big blisters had appeared. Some boys ran to inform their mother about the incident. Their mother was doing some work inside the house. Chandrashekhar's father Pandit Sitaram Tiwari was in the outer room. He heard the details of the incident from the children and rushed towards the spot. When the boy Chandrashekhar saw his father coming, he ran towards the forest. He thought that his father would beat him now. He stayed in the forest for three days. One day his mother came searching for him and brought him home. She assured him that his father would not say anything to him.

'Azad' When Mahatma Gandhi started the non-cooperation movement in 1921, he actively participated in it. Chandrashekhar was also caught while staging a sit-in one day. He was presented in the court of Parsi magistrate Mr. Khareghat. Mr. Khareghat used to give very harsh punishments. He started asking the boy Chandrashekhar about his personal information - "What is your name?" "My name is Azad." "What is your father's name?" "My father's name is Swadhin." "Where is your house?" "My house is the prison."

The magistrate Mr. Khareghat was irritated with these answers. He sentenced Chandrashekhar to fifteen lashes. At that time Chandrashekhar was only fourteen years old. The executioner hit the naked body of the child Chandrashekhar with the canes with all his might. With each cane, some skin would come off. Chandrashekhar was used to enduring pain since childhood. He kept on saying "Mahatma Gandhi ki Jai" or "Bharat Mata ki Jai" with every cane. When all the canes were hit, as per the prison rules, the jailer placed three annas on his palm. The child Chandrashekhar threw those annas on the jailer's face and ran out of the jail. As a result of passing this first ordeal without any honour, the child Chandrashekhar was felicitated by the citizens in the Gyanvapi locality of Banaras. Now he started being called Chandrashekhar Azad. The mind of the young Chandrashekhar Azad now turned away from non-violent means of liberating the country and towards armed revolution. At that time Banaras was a stronghold of revolutionaries. He came in contact with Manmathnath Gupta and Pranavesh Chatterjee and became a member of the revolutionary group. That group of revolutionaries was known as "Hindustan Prajatantr Sangh".

Chandrashekhar Azad first participated in a big campaign in the "Kakori Dacoity". The leader of this campaign was Ramprasad Bismil. At that time Chandrashekhar Azad was young and his nature was also very fickle. That is why Ramprasad Bismil used to call him Quick Silver. On 9 August 1925, the revolutionaries stopped the Saharanpur-Lucknow passenger train at a place called Kakori near Lucknow and looted the British treasury kept in it. Later, all the revolutionaries were caught one by one; but Chandrashekhar Azad never came into the hands of the police. Although he used to go to the police station in Jhansi and gossip with the policemen, the policemen never suspected that he could be the great revolutionary Chandrashekhar Azad. After the Kakori incident, he reorganized the group. Now it was named 'Hindustan Socialist Republican Association and Army'. Chandrashekhar was the commander of this new group. He kept moving around and secretly expanding the work of the party. During his days on the run, he also spent some time as a sadhu on the banks of a river near Jhansi.

Many revolutionaries of the Kakori case were sentenced to death and many were given long prison terms. Chandrashekhar Azad escaped and set up his base in Jhansi. In Jhansi, Chandrashekhar Azad got good protection from a revolutionary friend Master Rudranarayan Singh. In Jhansi itself, he found good friends in the form of Sadashiv Rao Malkapurkar, Bhagwandas Mahor and Vishwanath Vaishampayan. He worked as a motor mechanic for some days in Jhansi's 'Bundelkhand Motor Company', learned to drive a car and also got a driving license from the Superintendent of Police by driving his car. Ramanand, a driver of Bundelkhand

Motor Company, got a room rented for Chandrashekhar Azad in his own locality. Everything was going well; But sometimes some incidents disturbed the peace of the locality. Near Azad's room, another driver named Ramdayal lived with his family. Though Ramdayal was a good man, but when he would come home drunk at night, he would create a lot of ruckus and beat his wife a lot. The people of the locality felt very bad on hearing the woman cry; but they did not consider it appropriate to interfere in anyone's domestic matters. One day early in the morning, when Chandrashekhar Azad came out of his room to go to the factory, he met Ramdayal. Ramdayal started the conversation -

"Why Harishankar ji! (Azad had declared his name as Harishankar) these days you stay awake till late at night and keep banging and banging. Your banging disturbs our sleep. Though Azad wanted to avoid the situation, but the way Ramdayal had said it, he found it very good to reply and Azad gave a befitting reply to the brick - "Ramdayal bhai! I only beat up the machinery, but you keep disturbing the sleep of the entire neighbourhood by beating up your cow-like wife under the influence of alcohol." Ramdayal found this reply very harsh. He felt bad that someone should interfere in his domestic matters. His humanity vanished and his animality took over. Burning with anger, he burst out, "Why, you! Who are you to my wife that you are taking her side like this? I will beat her and beat her hard. Let's see who saves her." Azad replied to him calmly, "When you have called me brother-in-law, you have accepted that I am your wife's brother. A brother cannot see his sister being beaten. If you beat her at night under the influence of alcohol again, it will not be good." Ramdayal found the challenge unbearable. He lost his temper and shouted, "To hell with the night and the intoxication." I kill him on the road in broad daylight, without consuming any intoxicant. Let's see who comes forward to save her." Saying this, Ramdayal entered his house in anger and dragged his wife out by her hair and raised his hand to hit her. He could not even hit his wife with his hand when Azad caught his hand and pulled him towards himself. Due to this jerk, his wife's hair slipped from his hand and she was freed. Now Azad hit him hard on the cheek. Ramdayal's cheek was slapped so hard that darkness fell before his eyes and he sat down holding his head with both his hands. Meanwhile, people from the neighbourhood ran and some people took Azad inside the room while explaining to him. After this incident, Azad and Ramdayal stopped talking to each other for a few days, but Azad himself took the initiative and made his relations cordial with him and now started calling him "brother-in-law". Ramdayal never beat his wife again. Azad's reputation spread in the entire locality. Another incident similar to this also happened a few days ago. This happened in the interval. Which spread the fear of Azad in the whole of Jhansi.

When the police activity in Jhansi started increasing, Chandrashekhar Azad moved to Orchha state and built a hut on the banks of the Satar river and started living as a brahmachari. One secret of Azad not being caught was that in times of crisis, he would leave the city and move towards the villages and keep himself safe. By connecting the sources of Hindustan Samajwadi Prajatantra Sena Kranti, Chandrashekhar Azad now made a strong revolutionary organization. Now the name of his party was "Hindustan Samajwadi Prajatantra Sena". His comrades made him the "Commander of Chief" of this army. Now a revolutionary like Bhagat Singh was also his companion. The area of operation of this party increased to Uttar Pradesh and Punjab.

6. Bhagat Singh

Bhagat Singh was born on 28 September 1907 Death 23 March 1931 The slogan Inquilab Zindabad should be destroyed by imperialism.

Every particle of ashes is moving from my heat, I am such a madman who is free even in jail. It was not necessary that the revolution should be involved in the cursed struggle, it was not a cult of bombs and pistols. Bombs and pistols do not bring revolution, the sword of revolution is rubbed on a stone increasing the edge of ideas. Bhagat Singh Sandhu was born on 28 September 1907, but according to many evidences of the time, he was born on 19 October 1907 AD. His father's name was Sardar Kishan Singh and mother's name was Vidyavati Kaur. It was a Jat Sikh family. His family was completely Arya Samaji. The Jallianwala Bagh massacre in Amritsar on 13 April 1919 had a profound effect on the thinking of Bhagat Singh. After leaving the National College of Lahore, Bhagat Singh established the Naujawan Bharat Sabha for the independence of India. In the Kakori incident, Bhagat Singh was so agitated by the hanging of 4 revolutionaries including Ram Prasad 'Bismil' and the sentences of imprisonment to 16 others that his party Hindustan Republican Association along with Pandit Chandrashekhar Azad was so disturbed. and gave it a new name of Hindustan Socialist Republican Association. The purpose of this organization was to prepare youth who could suffer service, sacrifice and suffering. Bhagat Singh, along with Rajguru, killed the British officer JP Saunders, who was Assistant Superintendent of Police in Lahore on 17 December 1928. Revolutionary Chandrashekhar Azad had fully assisted him in this action. Bhagat Singh, along with revolutionary partner Batukeshwar Dutt, threw bombs and pamphlets to wake up the British government on 8 April 1929 in the Parliament House, the auditorium of the then Central Assembly of British India, in present-day New Delhi. After throwing the bomb, both of them also gave their arrest there. At that time Bhagat Singh was about twelve years old when the Jallianwala Bagh massacre took place. On getting information about this, Bhagat Singh reached Jallianwala Bagh after walking 12 miles from his school. At this age, Bhagat Singh used to read the revolutionary books of his uncles and think whether his path is right or not? After Gandhiji's non-cooperation movement broke out, he started choosing his way from Gandhiji's non-violent methods and the violent movement of revolutionaries. Due to the cancellation of Gandhiji's non-cooperation movement, there was some anger in him, but like the whole nation, he also respected Mahatma Gandhi. But instead of Gandhiji's non-violent movement, he did not consider it unreasonable to adopt the path of violent revolution for the freedom of the country. He started participating in the processions and became a member of many revolutionary parties. Among the main revolutionaries of his party were Chandrashekhar Azad, Sukhdev, Rajguru etc. Bhagat Singh was so disturbed by the hanging of 4 revolutionaries in the Kakori incident and the sentences of 16 others that he merged his party Naujawan Bharat Sabha with the Hindustan Republican Association in 1928. and gave him a new name

In 1928, there were fierce demonstrations to boycott the Simon Commission. The British government also lathi-charged the people participating in these demonstrations. Lala Lajpat Rai died due to injuries sustained in this lathi-charge. Now they could not hold themselves back. Under a secret plan, they planned to kill Police Superintendent Scott. According to the plan, Bhagat Singh and Rajguru started walking in a busy manner in front of Lahore Kotwali. On the other hand, Jai Gopal sat down with his bicycle as if it had broken down. Both became alert on Gopal's signal. On the other hand, Chandrashekhar Azad was hiding near the boundary wall of the nearby D.A.V. School and was acting as a guard to carry out the incident. On 17 December 1928, at around 4:15, as soon as ASP Saunders arrived, Rajguru shot him straight in the head, after which he lost consciousness immediately. After this, Bhagat Singh fired 3-4 bullets and made complete arrangements for his death. As soon as these two were running away, a soldier named Chanan Singh started chasing them. Chandrashekhar Azad warned him - "If you move ahead, I will shoot you." When he did not listen, Azad shot him. In this way these people avenged the death of Lala Lajpat Rai.

Although Bhagat Singh was not in favour of bloodshed, he believed in leftist ideology, and he was associated with the principles of Karl Marx and he was promoting the same ideology. Although, he was also a staunch supporter of socialism. Later, his opponents accused him of misleading the youth in the name of Bhagat Singh by telling them his ideology. Despite Congress being in power, Congress could not get Bhagat Singh the status of a martyr, because they only used the name of Bhagat Singh to connect the youth to their party. They did not like the policy of capitalists to exploit the workers. Since the British were all powerful at that time and very few Indian industrialists were able to make progress, their opposition to the British atrocities against workers was natural. It was their party's decision not to let such anti-labour policies be passed in the British Parliament. Everyone wanted the British to know that the Indians have woken up and they have anger in their hearts against such policies. To do this, they had planned to throw a bomb in the Central Assembly of Delhi. Bhagat Singh wanted that there should be no bloodshed in this and his 'voice' should reach the British.

Although initially not everyone in his group thought so, in the end the names of Bhagat Singh and Batukeshwar Dutt were unanimously chosen. As per the schedule, on 8 April 1929, both of them threw a bomb in the Central Assembly at a place where no one was present, otherwise he could have been hurt. The entire hall was filled with smoke. Bhagat Singh could have run away if he wanted, but he had already decided that he would accept the punishment even if it was hanging; hence he refused to run away. At that time both of them were wearing khaki shirts and shorts. After the bomb exploded, they shouted the slogan "Inquilab-Zindabad, Samrajyaavad-Murdabad!"[9] and threw the pamphlets they had brought with them in the air. Shortly after this, the police arrived and both of them were arrested.

Bhagat Singh remained in jail for about 2 years. During this time he kept expressing his revolutionary thoughts by writing articles. His studies continued while he was in jail. His articles written during that time and letters written to his relatives are still a mirror of his thoughts. In his articles, he has described the capitalists as his enemy in many ways. He wrote that the one who exploits the workers, even if he is an Indian, is his enemy. He also wrote an article in English in jail, titled Why am I an atheist? In jail, Bhagat Singh and his companions went on a hunger strike for 64 days. One of his companions, Jatindranath Das, even sacrificed his life in the hunger strike.

On 26 August 1930, the court convicted Bhagat Singh under Sections 129, 302 of the Indian Penal Code, Sections 4 and 6F of the Explosive Substances Act and Section 120 of the IPC. On 7 October 1930, the court gave a 68-page judgment, in which Bhagat Singh, Sukhdev and Rajguru were sentenced to death. With the death sentence being pronounced, Section 144 was imposed in Lahore. After this, an appeal was filed in the Privy Council for pardon of Bhagat Singh from death sentence but this appeal was rejected on 10 January 1931. After this, the then Congress President Pt. Madan Mohan Malviya filed an appeal before the Viceroy on 14 February 1931 for pardon of sentence that he should use his privilege and pardon the death sentence on humanitarian grounds. To get Bhagat Singh's death sentence pardoned, Mahatma Gandhi talked to the Viceroy on 17 February 1931 and then on 18 February 1931, an appeal was filed before the Viceroy on behalf of the general public with various arguments for pardon of sentence. All this was happening against the wishes of Bhagat Singh because Bhagat Singh did not want his sentence to be pardoned. On 23 March 1931, at around 7:33 pm, Bhagat Singh and his two companions Sukhdev and Rajguru were hanged. Before going to the gallows, he was reading Lenin's biography and when he was asked about his last wish, he said that he was reading Lenin's biography and he should be given time to complete it. It is said that when the jail officials informed him that the time for his hanging had come, he said - "Wait! First let one revolutionary meet the other." Then after a minute, he threw the book towards the roof and said - "Okay, now let's go." While going to the gallows, all three of them were singing merrily - Mera rang de Basanti Chola, Mera rang de. Mera rang de Basanti Chola. My rang de Basanti Chola. Fearing that some movement might erupt after the hanging, the British first cut his dead body into pieces and then filled it in sacks and took it to Ferozepur where he was burnt by pouring kerosene instead of ghee. When the villagers saw the fire burning, they came close. Fearing this, the British threw the half-burnt pieces of his body in the Sutlej river and fled. When the villagers came near, they collected the pieces of his dead body and cremated him properly. And Bhagat Singh became immortal forever. After this, people started considering Gandhi as responsible for his death along with the British. For this reason, when Gandhi was going to participate in the Lahore session of the Congress, people welcomed Gandhiji with black flags. Gandhi was also attacked at one or two places, but the police accompanying him in plain clothes saved him.

His thoughts can be gauged from the letters and articles written by him during his jail days. He expressed grief over the distances created in Indian society due to script (especially in the context of Punjabi's Gurmukhi and Shahmukhi and Hindi and Arabic and Urdu), caste and religion. He thought about the attack by an Indian on the weaker section of the society as seriously as the atrocities committed by an Englishman. Apart from Hindi, Urdu, Punjabi and English, Bhagat Singh also knew Bengali which he had learnt from Batukeshwar Dutt. He believed that his martyrdom would make the Indian people more agitated and this would hardly happen if he remained alive. This is why he refused to write an apology even after being sentenced to death. Bhagat Singh followed all the instructions given by Pandit Ram Prasad 'Bismil' in his autobiography. He also wrote a letter to the British government in which it was said that he should be considered a prisoner of war, a symbol of the war of Indians against the British government and should be shot dead instead of being hanged. In a letter sent to his brother Kultar on March 3 before his hanging, Bhagat Singh had written -

"They are always concerned about what is the new way of committing tyranny, and we are interested in seeing what is the limit of tyranny. Why should we be angry with the world, and why blame fate? Even if the whole world is the enemy, come! Let's fight."

7. Sukhdev Thapar

Birth on 15 May 1907

Death on 23 March 1931

Sukhdev, who shook the British rule with his revolutionary activities, was born on 15 May 1907 in Ludhiana city of Punjab. From his childhood, he saw the atrocities of the British rule in India and due to this he became a revolutionary to break the chains of slavery. According to Chaman Lal, a professor at Jawaharlal Nehru University and author of many books on revolutionaries, Sukhdev, a member of the Hindustan Socialist Republican Association, was filled with the spirit of patriotism. He used to instill the spirit of patriotism in the youth at the National College of Lahore and inspire them to jump into the freedom movement. As a skilled leader, he also used to tell the students studying in the college about the glorious past of India.

He started the Naujawan Bharat Sabha in Lahore along with other revolutionary comrades. This was an organisation that inspired the youth to join the freedom movement. According to historian Malti Malik, Sukhdev not only instilled the spirit of patriotism in the youth, but also actively participated in revolutionary activities himself. His name is prominently known for the incident of 1928 when the revolutionaries killed Deputy Superintendent of Police JP Saunders, an agent of the British government, to avenge the death of Lala Lajpat Rai. This incident shook the British Empire and the revolutionaries were hailed all over the country. The case of Saunders' murder was known as the 'Lahore Conspiracy'. Rajguru, Sukhdev and Bhagat Singh were sentenced to death in this case. On 23 March 1931, all three revolutionaries happily went to the gallows and created a new urge for freedom in the minds of the youth of the country. Sukhdev was only 24 years old at the time of his martyrdom.

8. Rajguru

Birth on 24 August 1908

Death on 23 March 1931

Many revolutionaries have sacrificed their lives for our country to free India from slavery. It is because of the sacrifice of these revolutionaries that our country could become a free country. There are countless names of revolutionaries in the list of names of revolutionaries of our country and one of the names of these revolutionaries is also of 'Rajguru' ji. Who sacrificed his life for our country at a very young age and his sacrifice is still remembered by the people of India. Today, through this article, we are going to tell you what sacrifices Rajguru ji had made for India and how he became a great revolutionary.

Shivram Hari Rajguru belonged to the Maharashtra state of India and was born in a simple family in this state in 1908. The village in Pune city of Maharashtra where he was born was named Khed. Rajguru ji spent his childhood in this village. Rajguru ji's father Hari Narayan had two marriages. He had a total of 6 children from his first marriage and he married Parvati ji for the second time and he had five children from this marriage and Rajguru ji was his fifth child. Rajguru ji belonged to a Brahmin family and according to the information available in history, Rajguru ji was raised by his mother Parvati Bai and his elder brother. Because when he was just 6 years old, his father Hari Narayan died at that time.

Rajguru ji belonged to a Brahmin family and according to the information available in history, Rajguru ji was raised by his mother Parvati Bai and his elder brother. Because when he was just 6 years old, his father Hari Narayan died. When Rajguru ji was getting his education in Varanasi, he met some revolutionaries of our country. Who were fighting to free our country from the British. After meeting these revolutionaries, Rajguru ji also got involved in the struggle to free our country and he joined the Hindustan Socialist Republican Association (HSRA) in the year 1924. This association was a revolutionary organization, which was formed by Chandrashekhar Azad, Bhagat Singh, Sukhdev Thapar and other revolutionaries. The goal of HSRA was only related to the independence of the country. As a member of this association, Rajguru ji went to cities like Punjab, Agra, Lahore and Kanpur and worked to connect the people there with his association. At the same time, within a very short time, Rajguru ji also became a very good friend of Bhagat Singh ji and both these heroes together carried out many movements against British India.

In the year 1928, Rajguru ji took revenge from the British for the murder of India's famous revolutionary Lala Lajpat Rai. In fact, in the same year, British India appointed the 'Simon Commission' to look into the issue of political reforms in India. But not a single Indian leader was included in this commission. Due to which the angry Indian nationalist leaders boycotted this commission and Lala Lajpat Rai died in a lathi charge during this boycott. After the death of

Lala Lajpat Rai, Rajguru ji, Bhagat Singh ji and Chandrashekhar Azad ji together resolved to take revenge for this murder. In their resolution, they had planned to kill Superintendent of Police James A Scott. Because the lathi charge was done on the orders of James A Scott, in which Rai ji died. According to the strategy made by Rajguru ji and his companions, revolutionary Jai Gopal had to identify Scott. Because Rajguru ji and his companions did not recognize Scott. To execute this plan, they chose the day of 17 December, 1928. On 17 December, Rajguru and Bhagat Singh were waiting for Scott outside the district police headquarters in Lahore. Meanwhile, Jai Gopal pointed towards a police officer and told them that he was Stock and as soon as they got the signal, they shot and killed that person. But the person Jai Gopal pointed towards was not Stock but John P Saunders who was an Assistant Commissioner. After the murder of John P Saunders, the British started an exercise to catch his killers all over India. It is said that the British knew that Bhagat Singh was behind the murder of P Saunders and on the basis of this suspicion, the police started the work of catching Bhagat Singh. To escape from the British, Bhagat Singh and Rajguru decided to leave Lahore and prepared a strategy to get out of this city. To make their strategy successful, both of them took the help of Durga Devi Vohra. Durga ji was the wife of revolutionary Bhagwati Charan. According to their strategy, they had to catch the train going from Lahore to Howrah. Bhagat Singh had completely changed his disguise so that he would not be recognized by the British. After changing his disguise, Singh boarded the train with Vohra and his child. Apart from Bhagat ji, Rajguru ji also boarded the train after changing his disguise. When the train reached Lucknow, Rajguru ji got down there and left for Banaras. Bhagat Singh ji headed towards Howrah with Vohra and his child.

After living in Uttar Pradesh for some time, Rajguru ji went to Nagpur. Here he took shelter in the house of an RSS worker. On 30 September 1929, when he was going from Nagpur to Pune, he was caught by the British. Apart from this, the British also arrested Bhagat ji and Sukhdev Thapar ji. Rajguru ji was hanged in the year 1931 after being found guilty in the murder of Saunders. Sukhdev ji and Bhagat Singh ji were also given this punishment along with him. In this way, our country lost three revolutionaries of its country on 23 March. At the time when Rajguru ji was crucified by the British, he was only 22 years old.

9. Dr Bhimrao Ambedkar

Birth on April 14, 1891

Death on December 6, 1956

Anmol Vichar

I believe in a religion which teaches liberty, equality and fraternity.

History shows that where there is a conflict between morality and economics, economics always wins. Vested interests are not willingly given up unless sufficient force is applied to compel.

A great man differs from an eminent man in that he is willing to be the servant of society.

There is no scope for the development of conscience, reason and independent thinking in Hinduism.

Unless you achieve social freedom, whatever freedom the law gives you is of no use to you.

Bhimrao Ramji Ambedkar, popularly known as Babasaheb Ambedkar, was an Indian polymath, jurist, economist, politician, and social reformer. He inspired the Dalit Buddhist movement and campaigned against social discrimination against the untouchables (Dalits). He also supported the rights of workers, peasants and women. He was the first Law and Justice Minister of independent India, the father of the Indian Constitution and the architect of the Republic of India. Ambedkar was a brilliant student. He received doctorates in economics from both Columbia University and the London School of Economics and also did research work in law, economics and political science. In the early part of his professional life, he was a professor of economics and also practiced law and later life was more devoted to political activities. Bhimrao then became involved in the campaign and discussions for the independence of India and contributed significantly to the creation of India by publishing magazines, advocating political rights and social freedoms for Dalits. In 1956, he converted to Buddhism. In 1990, he was posthumously awarded the Bharat Ratna, India's highest civilian honor. Ambedkar's legacy includes numerous memorials and depictions in popular culture.

Ambedkar was born on 14 April 1891 in the Mhow Nagar Military Cantonment in the Central India Province (now Madhya Pradesh) of British India. He was the 14th and last child of Ramji Maloji Sakpal and Bhimabai. His family was of Marathi origin and was a resident of Ambadve village in Ratnagiri district of present-day Maharashtra. He belonged to the Hindu Mahar caste, which was then considered untouchable and due to this he had to endure severe social and economic discrimination. Bhimrao Ambedkar's ancestors had served in the British East India Company's army for a long time and his father Ramji Sakpal served in the Mhow Cantonment of the Indian Army and while working here he reached the rank of Subedar. He received formal education in Marathi and English.

Due to his caste, the child Bhim was facing social resistance. Despite being capable of studying in school, student Bhimrao had to face many difficulties due to untouchability. Ramji Ambedkar remarried Jijabai in 1898. On 7 November 1900, Ramji Sakpal enrolled his son Bhimrao's name as Bhiva Ramji Ambavadekar in the Government High School of Satara. Bhiva was his childhood name. Ambedkar's original surname was Ambedvekar instead of Sakpal, which was related to his village Ambedve. Since people of Konkan province used to keep their surname from the name of the village, Ambedkar's surname Ambedvekar from his village Ambedve was enrolled in the school. Later, a Devrukhe Brahmin teacher Krishna Mahadev Ambedkar, who had special affection for him, removed 'Ambedkar' from his name and added his simple 'Ambedkar' surname, since then he is known by the name Ambedkar. Ramabai Ambedkar, Ambedkar's wife Ramji Sakpal moved to Bombay with the family. In April 1906, when Bhimrao was about 15 years old, he was married to Ramabai, a nine-year-old girl. He was then studying in the fifth English class. Child marriage was prevalent in India in those days.

Ambedkar took admission in the first class of English on 7 November 1900 in the Government High School (now Pratap Singh High School) located at Rajwada Chowk in Satara city. His educational life started from this day, so 7 November is celebrated as Students' Day in Maharashtra. At that time he was called 'Bhiva'. At that time in the school, his name was recorded in the attendance register as 'Bhiva Ramji Ambedkar' at number - 1914. When he passed the English fourth class examination, since this was an unusual thing among the untouchables, Bhimrao's success was celebrated among the untouchables and in a public ceremony, and his family friend and writer Dada Keluskar presented him with a 'Biography of the Buddha' written by himself. After reading this, he came to know about Gautam Buddha and Buddhism for the first time and was influenced by their teachings. In 1897, Ambedkar's family moved to Mumbai where he received further education at the Government High School on Elphinstone Road. Undergraduate studies at Bombay University Ambedkar as a student In 1907, he passed his matriculation examination and the following year he entered Elphinstone College, which was affiliated with the University of Bombay. He was the first from his community to receive education at this level. By 1912, he received a Bachelor of Arts (B.A.) in economics and political science from Bombay University, and began working with the Baroda state government. His wife had just moved their new family in and started work when she had to return to Mumbai to see her ailing father, who died on 2 February 1913.

In 1913, Ambedkar moved to the United States at the age of 22 where he was awarded a Baroda State Scholarship of $11.50 per month for three years under a scheme established by Sayajirao Gaekwad III (Gaekwad of Baroda) to provide opportunities for postgraduate education at Columbia University in New York City. Soon after arriving there he settled with a Parsi friend, Naval Bhathena, at Livingston Hall. In June 1915 he passed his Master of Arts (M.A.) examination, with economics as his major subject and sociology, history, philosophy and anthropology as his other subjects. He submitted his thesis for the Masters on the subject of Commerce in Ancient Indians. Ambedkar was influenced by John Dewey and his work on democracy. In 1916, he was awarded a second Master of Arts for his thesis, National Dividend of India – A Historical and Analytical Study, and eventually set off for London. In 1916 he received a PhD in economics for his third thesis, Evolution of Provincial Finance in British India, and was officially awarded in 1927 after publishing his thesis. On 9 May, he presented a paper titled Castes in India: Their System, Origin, and Development, his first published paper, at a seminar organized by anthropologist Alexander Goldenweiser. He used the scholarship for a period of three years to complete the course in America in just two years and went to London in 1916.

In October 1916, he went to London and joined Gray's Inn for the barrister course (law studies), and also joined the London School of Economics where he began working on his doctoral thesis in economics. In June 1917, he was forced to temporarily abandon his studies and return to India as his scholarship from the Baroda state was terminated. On his return, his book collection was sent on a different ship from the one that was sunk by a German submarine torpedo. This was the period of World War I. He was allowed to return to London to complete his thesis within four years. While working as the military secretary of the Baroda state, Dr. Bhimrao Ambedkar was disheartened by the discrimination that suddenly reappeared in his life and left his job and started working as a private tutor and accountant. He even started his own consultancy business which failed due to his social status. Through one of his English acquaintances, Lord Sydenham, a former Governor of Bombay, he got a job as Professor of Political Economy at the Sydenham College of Commerce and Economics in Bombay. In 1920, with the help of Shahu Maharaj of Kolhapur, his Parsi friend and some personal savings, he was able to return to England once again and obtained a Master of Science (M.Sc.) in 1921. In 1922, he was awarded the degree of Barrister-at-Law by Gray's Inn and was admitted to the British Bar as a barrister. In 1923, he obtained a D.Sc. (Doctor of Science) in Economics. His thesis was on "The Problem of the Rupee: Its Origin and Its Solution". Returning to India after completing his studies in London, Bhimrao Ambedkar stayed in Germany for three months, where he continued his study of economics at the University of Bonn. But due to lack of time, he could not stay in the university for long. His third and fourth doctorates (LL.D., Columbia University, 1952 and D.Litt., Osmania University, 1953) were honorary degrees.

Ambedkar said "Untouchability is worse than slavery." Ambedkar was educated by the princely state of Baroda and was obliged to serve them. He was appointed military secretary to Maharaja Gaekwad, but was forced to leave the job soon after due to caste discrimination. He described this incident in his autobiography, Waiting for a Visa. Subsequently, he tried again to find a livelihood for his growing family, working as an accountant, a private tutor, and setting up an investment consultancy business, but all these efforts failed when his clients learned that he was an untouchable. In 1918, he became a professor of political economy at the Sydenham College of Commerce and Economics in Mumbai. Although he was successful with students, other professors objected to him sharing drinking vessels with them. Ambedkar was invited to testify as one of India's leading scholars before the Southborough Committee, which was preparing the Government of India Act 1919. During this hearing, Ambedkar advocated separate electorates and reservations for Dalits and other religious communities. In 1920, from Bombay, he began publishing the weekly Mooknayak. The publication soon became popular among readers, and Ambedkar used it to criticise orthodox Hindu politicians and the Indian political community's reluctance to fight caste discrimination. His speech at a conference of the Dalit class greatly impressed Shahu IV, the local ruler of Kolhapur state, whose dining with Ambedkar caused a stir in conservative society. While practising law in the Bombay High Court, he made efforts to promote the education of the untouchables and uplift them. His first organised effort was the establishment of the central institution Bahishkrit Hitakarini Sabha, aimed at promoting education and socio-economic reform as well as the welfare of the "outcasts", also referred to as the depressed classes. To protect Dalit rights, he started five magazines, namely Mooknayak, Bahishkrit Bharat, Samata, Prabuddha Bharat and Janata.

In 1925, he was appointed to serve on the all-European Simon Commission in the Bombay Presidency Committee. There were protests all over India against the commission. While its report was ignored by most Indians, Ambedkar separately wrote recommendations for future constitutional reforms. Dr. Babasaheb Ambedkar and his followers at 'Jaystambh', Koregaon Bhima, 1 January 1927 On 1 January 1927, Ambedkar organized a ceremony at the Koregaon Vijay Smarak (Jaystambh) to honour the Indian Mahar soldiers who died during the Battle of Koregaon on 1 January 1818 as part of the Second Anglo-Maratha War. Here the names of the soldiers belonging to the Mahar community were engraved on a marble plaque and Koregaon was made a symbol of Dalit self-respect.

By 1927, Dr. Ambedkar decided to launch a widespread and active movement against untouchability. Through public movements, satyagrahas and processions, he fought to open public resources of drinking water to all sections of the society and also to give the untouchables the right to enter Hindu temples. He also led a satyagraha in the city of Mahad to get the untouchable community the right to take water from the city's Chavdar pond. At a conference in late 1927, Ambedkar publicly denounced the ancient Hindu text, the Manusmriti, for ideologically justifying caste discrimination and "untouchability", and he ceremonially burned copies of the ancient text. On 25 December 1927, he led thousands of followers in burning copies of the Manusmriti. To commemorate this, 25 December is celebrated every year by Ambedkarites and Hindu Dalits as Manusmriti Dahan Diwas. In 1930, Ambedkar launched the Kalaram Mandir Satyagraha after three months of preparation. The Kalaram Mandir movement gathered about 15,000 volunteers, leading to one of the largest processions in Nashik. The procession was led by a military band, a batch of scouts, women and men walked in discipline, order and determination to see the Lord for the first time. When they reached the gates, the gates were closed by Brahmin officials.

By now Bhimrao Ambedkar had become the greatest untouchable political figure of all time. He bitterly criticised the major mainstream political parties for their alleged indifference towards the abolition of the caste system. Ambedkar also criticised the Indian National Congress and its leader Mahatma Gandhi, accusing them of presenting the untouchable community as an object of pity. Ambedkar was also dissatisfied with the failures of British rule, and advocated a separate political identity for the untouchable community in which there would be no interference from either the Congress or the British. During the first Round Table Conference, a conference of the oppressed class held on 8 August 1930 in London, Ambedkar presented his political vision to the world, according to which the security of the oppressed class lies in its independence from both the government and the Congress. We have to make our own way and do it ourselves... Political power cannot be the solution to the problems of the oppressed; their salvation lies in finding their rightful place in society. They must change their bad way of living... they must be educated... There is a great need to shake off their feeling of inferiority and to establish in them that divine discontent which is the source of all heights. Ambedkar criticized the Salt Satyagraha launched by the Congress and Gandhi. Due to his growing popularity and public support among the untouchable community, he was invited to participate in the second Round Table Conference to be held in London in 1931. There he had a heated debate with Gandhi on the issue of giving a separate electorate to the untouchables. But Dr. Ambedkar agreed with Ambedkar's views. Gandhi, a strong opponent of giving a separate electorate on the basis of religion and caste, feared that a separate electorate given to the untouchables would divide the Hindu society. Gandhi felt that some period of change of heart should be given to the upper castes to make them forget untouchability, but this argument proved wrong when the upper caste Hindus continued to practice untouchability even decades after the Poona Pact.

M.R. Jayakar, Tej Bahadur and Dr. Ambedkar in Yerwada Central Jail on 24 September 1932. In 1932, the British agreed with Ambedkar's ideas and announced a separate electorate for the untouchables. The announcement of the Communal Award was the result of the discussions held in the Round Table Conference. Under this agreement, the demand for political representation raised by Ambedkar was accepted and the Dalit class was given the right of two votes in a separate electorate. Under this, the Dalits could choose their representative with one vote and had the freedom to choose the representative of the general class with the second vote. In this way, the Dalit representative was to be elected only with the votes of the Dalits. With this provision, the general category had no say in the selection of the Dalit representative. But the Dalit class could play its role by using its second vote to elect a representative of the general category. In such a situation, the Dalit candidate elected by the Dalits could put forward the problems of the Dalits well, but it was not necessary for the non-Dalit candidate to even try to solve their problems. Gandhi was in Pune's Yerwada jail at this time. As soon as the Communal Award was announced, Gandhi first wrote a letter to the Prime Minister demanding its change. But when he felt that no action was being taken on his demand, he announced to observe a fast unto death. Then Ambedkar said that "It would have been good if Gandhi had observed this fast for the independence of the country, but he has observed this fast against the Dalit people, which is very regrettable. Whereas there was no objection from Gandhi's side regarding this right (of separate election) given to Indian Christians, Muslims and Sikhs." He also said that Gandhi is not an immortal person. Who knows how many such people were born and died in India. Ambedkar said that he cannot sacrifice the interests of Dalits to save Gandhi's life. Now due to the fast unto death, Gandhi's health was continuously deteriorating. Gandhi's life was in grave danger. And the entire Hindu society became opposed to Ambedkar.

Seeing the increasing pressure in the country, Ambedkar reached Yerwada Jail on 24 September 1932 at 5 pm. Here an agreement was reached between Gandhi and Ambedkar, which later came to be known as the Poona Pact. In this agreement, Ambedkar announced to give up the right of separate election given to Dalits in the Communal Award. But along with this, instead of the 78 reserved seats given by the Communal Award, the number of reserved seats in the Poona Pact was increased to 148. Along with this, a sufficient amount was fixed in the education grant for untouchables in every province and recruitment of people of Dalit class was ensured without any discrimination in government jobs and in this way Ambedkar saved the life of Mahatma

Gandhi. Ambedkar was not satisfied with this agreement, he termed Gandhi's fast as a drama played by Gandhi to deprive the untouchables of their political rights and to pressurize them to withdraw from their demand. In 1942, Ambedkar condemned this agreement. In his book 'State of Minority', he expressed his displeasure over the Poona Pact. The Republican Party of India has also held condemnation meetings many times before this.

Ambedkar's grandfather's name was Maloji Sakpal, his father's name was Ramji Sapkal and mother's name was Bhimabai. In 1906, when Ambedkar was five years old, his mother died. Therefore, his aunt Mirabai, who was his father's elder sister, took care of him. On Mirabai's insistence, Ramji remarried Jijabai so that the child Bhimrao could get mother's love. Prakash, Anandraj and Bhimrao, all three are sons of Yashwant Ambedkar. Ambedkar was married to Ramabai when he was studying in the fifth English class. Ramabai and Bhimrao also had five children - four sons: Yashwant, Ramesh, Gangadhar, Rajratna and one daughter: Indu. But except Yashwant, all the children died in childhood. Ambedkar considered three great people as his gurus. His first guru was Tathagata Gautam Buddha, the second was Sant Kabir and the third guru was Mahatma Jyotiba Phule.

On 13 October 1935, Ambedkar was appointed Principal of the Government Law College, a position he held for two years. He also served as the President of the Governing Body of Delhi University's Ramjas College after the death of its founder, Shri Rai Kedar Nath.[49] Ambedkar settled in Bombay (now Mumbai), where he built a three-storey house called Rajgriha, which housed his private library of over 50,000 books, then the largest private library in the world.[50] On 27 May 1935, his wife Ramabai died after a prolonged illness. Ramabai wanted to go on a pilgrimage to Pandharpur before her death, but Ambedkar did not allow her to do so. Ambedkar said that there was no point in going to a Hindu pilgrimage where they were considered untouchables, instead he talked about building a new Pandharpur for them. In 1936, Ambedkar founded the Independent Labour Party, which won 15 seats in the 1937 Central Legislative Assembly elections. In the same year, Ambedkar published his book 'Annihilation of Caste' on 15 May 1936, which was based on a research paper he had written in New York. In this book, Ambedkar strongly criticized Hindu religious leaders and the caste system. [53] He strongly condemned the Congress' decision to call people of untouchable community Harijans, a term coined by Gandhi. Later, in a 1955 BBC interview, he accused Gandhi of supporting the caste system in his Gujarati language papers and opposing the caste system in his English language papers.

Ambedkar served on the Defence Advisory Committee and as Labour Minister for the Viceroy's Executive Council during 1942–1946. Ambedkar actively participated in India's struggle for independence. Following the Muslim League's Lahore Resolution (1940) demanding Pakistan, Ambedkar wrote a 400-page book called "Thoughts on Pakistan", which analysed the concept of "Pakistan" in all its aspects. In it, he criticised the Muslim League's demand for a separate country for Muslims, Pakistan, and argued that Hindus should accept a Pakistan for Muslims. He proposed that the provincial boundaries of Punjab and Bengal should be redrawn to separate Muslim and non-Muslim majority parts. He thought that Muslims could have no objection to the redrawing of provincial boundaries. If they did, they "did not quite understand the nature of their demand". Scholar Venkat Dhaliwal states that Thoughts on Pakistan "preoccupied Indian politics for a decade". It set the course of dialogue between the Muslim League and the Indian National Congress, paving the way for the partition of India.[58] Though he was a strong critic of Muhammad Ali Jinnah and the Muslim League's divisive communal strategy, he argued that Hindus and non-Muslims should have a common goal of achieving Pakistan. Muslims should be separated and Pakistan should be formed because ethnic nationalism leading a single country would lead to more violence within the country. He cited historical events such as the dissolution of the Ottoman Empire and Czechoslovakia to support his view about the communal division of Hindus and Muslims. He asked whether there were sufficient reasons for the creation of Pakistan and suggested that the differences between Hindus and Muslims could have been resolved with a less drastic step. He wrote that Pakistan must justify its existence. Communal issues have always existed in countries like Canada, but even today the British and the French live together, so can't Hindus and Muslims live together? He warned that the actual implementation of the solution of creating two countries would be extremely difficult. There would also be the problem of border disputes along with the migration of a large population. This prediction was correct in view of the violence that followed India's independence.

With this book, "What Congress and Gandhi Have Done to the Untouchables?", Ambedkar sharpened his attacks on both Gandhi and the Congress, accusing them of hypocrisy. Ambedkar transformed his political party into the All India Scheduled Caste Federation, which fared poorly in the 1946 elections to the Constituent Assembly of India. He was later elected to the Constituent Assembly from Bengal, where the Muslim League was in power.[61] Ambedkar contested the first Indian general election of 1952 from Bombay North, but lost to his former assistant and Congress Party candidate Narayan Kajolkar. Ambedkar became a member of the Rajya Sabha, presumably an appointed member. He tried to enter the Lok Sabha again in a 1954 by-election from Bhandara, but finished third (the Congress Party won). By the time of the second general election in 1957, Ambedkar had passed away. In his book Who Were the Shudras?, he explained how the Shudras, the lowest caste in the hierarchy of the Hindu caste system, came into being. He also emphasised how the Atishudras (untouchables) were different from the Shudras. In his 1948 sequel to Who Were the Shudras?, The Untouchables: A Thesis on the Origin of Untouchability, Ambedkar lashed out at Hinduism. Hindu civilization ... is a cruel device for enslaving and suppressing humanity and its proper name would be infamy. What more can be said about a civilization which has developed a very large class of people who are considered ... less than a human being and whose mere touch is sufficient reason to spread pollution? Ambedkar was also a great critic of the practices of Islam in South Asia. He supported the partition of India but strongly condemned the practice of child marriage and the ill treatment of women among Muslims. He said,

Words cannot express the evils of polygamy and keeping concubines which are the source of misery of a Muslim woman in particular. Take the caste system, everybody says that Islam should be free from slavery and caste, whereas slavery exists and has found support in Islam and Islamic countries. While the prescriptions of the Prophet regarding justice and humane treatment of slaves contained in the Quran are laudable, there is nothing in Islam that supports the abolition of this curse. Even if slavery is abolished, the caste system will still remain among Muslims. He wrote that Muslim society has more social evils than Hindu society and Muslims hide them by using soft words like "brotherhood". He also criticized the discrimination by Muslims against the

Arzal classes who were considered "inferior" as well as the oppressive practice of purdah which oppressed women in Muslim society. He said that although purdah is also prevalent among Hindus, it is only the Muslims who have given it religious recognition. He criticized the fanaticism in Islam due to which the society has become very rigid and it has become very difficult to change it due to the commitment to follow the principles of Islam in letter and spirit. He further wrote that Indian Muslims have failed to reform their society, while countries like Turkey, on the contrary, have changed themselves a lot. Both Hindus and Muslims, suffering from "communalism", have ignored the demand for social justice.

While living under Hindu religion for 10-12 years, Babasaheb Ambedkar made all efforts to reform Hindu religion and Hindu society, to achieve equality and respect, but the hearts of upper caste Hindus did not change. On the contrary, he was condemned and even called the destroyer of Hindu religion. After that he said, "We made every kind of effort and satyagraha to achieve the level of equality in Hindu society, but all proved futile. There is no place for equality in Hindu society." Hindu society used to say that "humans are for religion" while Ambedkar believed that "religion is for humans." Ambedkar said that there is no meaning in a religion in which there is no value of humanity. There is no meaning in living in a religion which does not allow the followers of its own religion (untouchables) to get religious education, hinders them in getting jobs, insults them on every small thing and does not even allow them to get water. Ambedkar did not announce his renunciation of Hinduism out of any kind of hostility or destruction of Hinduism, but he made this decision over some fundamental principles which were absolutely incompatible with Hinduism.

Despite bitter criticism of Gandhi and the Congress, Ambedkar's reputation as a unique scholar and jurist was such that when, after India's independence on 15 August 1947, the new Congress-led government came into being, it invited Ambedkar to serve as the country's first Minister of Law and Justice, which he accepted. On 29 August 1947, Ambedkar was appointed chairman of the Constitution Drafting Committee to draft the new Constitution of independent India. Ambedkar's study of early Buddhist Sangha practices and other Buddhist texts also helped in this task. Granville Austin described the Indian Constitution drafted by Ambedkar as 'the first and most important social document'. 'Most of India's constitutional provisions have been reached either in furtherance of the objective of social revolution or in an attempt to promote this revolution by establishing the conditions necessary for its achievement.' The text of the Constitution drafted by Ambedkar provided constitutional guarantees and protections for a wide range of civil liberties for individual citizens, including freedom of religion, the abolition of untouchability, and the outlawing of all forms of discrimination. Ambedkar argued for extensive economic and social rights for women, and won the Assembly's support for introducing a system of reservations of jobs in the civil services, schools and colleges for members of the Scheduled Castes (SCs) and Scheduled Tribes (STs) and Other Backward Classes (OBCs), which was an act of affirmative action. India's lawmakers hoped to eliminate socio-economic inequalities and lack of opportunities for India's depressed classes through these measures. The Constitution was adopted by the Constituent Assembly on 26 November 1949. Speaking after completing his work, Ambedkar said:

I feel that the Constitution is workable, flexible and yet strong enough to hold the country together in times of peace and war. In fact, I can say that if anything ever goes wrong, it will not be because our Constitution was bad but because the man who used it was mean.

Ambedkar opposed Article 370 of the Constitution of India, which gave special status to the state of Jammu and Kashmir, and which was included in the Constitution against his wishes. Balraj Madhok states that Ambedkar clearly told Kashmiri leader Sheikh Abdullah: "You want that India should protect your borders, it should build roads in your territory, it should supply you with grain, and Kashmir should be given the same status as India. But the Government of India should have only limited powers and the Indian people should have no rights in Kashmir. To give assent to this proposal, as the Law Minister of India, would be a treacherous thing against the interests of India, it would never do." Abdullah then approached Nehru, who directed him to Gopal Swami Ayyangar, who in turn approached Vallabhbhai Patel and said that Nehru had promised Sheikh Abdullah special status. Patel got the article passed while Nehru was on a foreign tour. The day the article came up for discussion, Ambedkar did not answer questions on it but participated on other articles. All arguments were made by Krishna Swami Ayyangar.

Ambedkar was actually in favour of Uniform Civil Code and opposed Article 370 in the case of Kashmir. Ambedkar's India would have been a country of modern, scientific thinking and rational ideas, there would be no place for personal law in it. [During the debate in the Constituent Assembly, Ambedkar expressed his desire to reform Indian society by recommending the adoption of a Uniform Civil Code. Ambedkar resigned from the cabinet in 1951 after his draft of the Hindu Code Bill was blocked in Parliament. The Hindu Code Bill was said to provide many rights to Indian women. This draft demanded gender equality in the laws of succession, marriage and economy. [Although Prime Minister Nehru, the cabinet and some other Congress leaders supported it, a large number of members of Parliament, including President Rajendra Prasad and Vallabhbhai Patel, were against it. Ambedkar contested the Lok Sabha elections from Bombay (North Central) constituency in 1952 as an independent candidate but he lost. In this election, Ambedkar got 123,576 votes and Narayan Sadoba Kajolkar got 138,137 votes. In March 1952, he was appointed to the upper house of Parliament i.e. Rajya Sabha and after that he remained a member of this house till his death.

Ambedkar was the first Indian to get a doctorate degree in economics from abroad. He argued that industrialization and agricultural development can lead to growth in the Indian economy. He emphasized investment in agriculture as the primary industry in India. According to Sharad Pawar, Ambedkar's philosophy helped the government achieve its food security goals. Ambedkar advocated national economic and social development, emphasizing education, public sanitation, community health, and residential facilities as basic amenities. He calculated the loss of development caused by British rule.

Reserve Bank of India

Ambedkar was trained as an economist, and by 1921 was a professional economist. When he became a political leader, he wrote three scholarly books on economics:

Administration and Finance of the East India

The Evaluation of Provincial Finance in British India

The Problem of the Rupee: Its Origin and Its Solution

The Reserve Bank of India (RBI) was based on Ambedkar's ideas, which he presented to the Hilton Young Commission

Ambedkar's first wife, Ramabai, died in 1935 after a long illness. After completing the draft of the Indian Constitution in the late 1940s, he suffered from sleep deprivation, had neuropathic pain in his legs, and was taking insulin and homeopathic medicines. He went to Bombay (Mumbai) for treatment, and there met Dr. Sharda Kabir, whom he married on 15 April 1948 at his home in New Delhi. The doctors recommended a life partner who was a good cook and had medical knowledge to take care of him. Dr. Sharda Kabir adopted the name Savita Ambedkar after marriage and took care of him for the rest of his life. Savita Ambedkar, who was called 'Mai' or 'Maisaaheb', died on 29 May 2003 in Mehrauli, New Delhi, at the age of 93.

In the 1950s, Bhimrao Ambedkar became attracted to Buddhism and went to Sri Lanka (then Ceylon) to attend a conference of Buddhist monks and scholars. While dedicating a new Buddhist Vihara near Pune, Dr. Ambedkar announced that he was writing a book on Buddhism and would formally convert to Buddhism as soon as it was finished. In 1954, Ambedkar visited Myanmar twice; the second time he went to Rangoon to attend the third World Buddhist Fellowship conference. In 1955 he founded the Bharatiya Bauddh Mahasabha i.e. the Buddhist Society of India. He completed his last famous work, The Buddha and His Dhamma in 1956. It was published after his death in 1957. In the preface of this book, Ambedkar wrote,

I consider the Dhamma of Buddha to be the best. No religion can be compared with it. If a modern man who believes in science should have any religion, it can only be Buddhism. This conviction has grown in me after twenty-five years of close study of all religions.

On 14 October 1956, Dr. Bhimrao Ambedkar organized a formal public conversion ceremony for himself and his supporters in the city of Nagpur. First, Dr. Ambedkar, along with his wife Savita and some companions, embraced Buddhism by adopting the Triratna and Panchsheel in the traditional way by the monk Mahasthavir Chandramani. After this, he converted his 5,00,000 followers to Navayana Buddhism by giving Triratna, Panchsheel and 22 vows. He was breaking the network of gods and imagining a free man who was religious but did not consider inequality as a value of life. In order to completely break the bonds of Hinduism, Ambedkar himself determined 22 vows for his Buddhist followers, which is an essence and philosophy of Buddhism. These vows were related to disbelief in the trinity of Hinduism, refutation of incarnation, abandonment of Shraddha-Tarpan, Pinddaan, belief in the principles and teachings of Buddha, not participating in any ceremony performed by Brahmins, belief in equality of man, following the Eightfold Path of Buddha, kindness towards creatures, not stealing, not lying, not consuming alcohol, abandoning the Hindu religion based on inequality and adopting Buddhism. By adopting Navayana, Ambedkar and his supporters clearly condemned and abandoned the inequality-based Hindu religion and Hindu philosophy. Ambedkar again initiated 2 to 3 lakh of his followers into Buddhism on the next day, 15 October, these were the followers who could not reach the ceremony of 14 October or reached late. Ambedkar initiated about 8 lakh people into Buddhism in Nagpur, hence this land became famous as Deekshabhoomi. On the third day, 16 October, Ambedkar went to Chandrapur and there also he initiated about 3,00,000 supporters into Buddhism. Thus, in just three days, Ambedkar himself converted more than 11 lakh people to Buddhism, increasing the number of Buddhists in the world by 11 lakh and reviving Buddhism in India. This event received congratulations from many people and Buddhist countries. After this, he went to Kathmandu to participate in the Fourth World Buddhist Conference in Nepal. There he visited the Dalit settlements of Kathmandu city. The Ambedkarite movement of Nepal is run by Dalit leaders, and most of the Dalit leaders of Nepal believe that only "Ambedkar's philosophy" is capable of eradicating caste discrimination. He completed his last manuscript, Buddha or Karl Marx, on 2 December 1956.

Since 1948, Ambedkar had been suffering from diabetes. He was seriously ill from June to October 1954, during which time he suffered from failing eyesight. Ambedkar's health deteriorated and he was exhausted by his political issues and his continuous work during 1955 left him exhausted. On 6 December 1956, three days after completing his last manuscript, The Buddha and His Dhamma, Ambedkar passed away in his sleep at his home in Delhi. He was then aged 64 years and 7 months. His body was brought to his home, Rajgriha in Mumbai, by a special flight from Delhi. On 7 December, he was cremated in a Buddhist style at the Dadar Chowpatty beach in Mumbai, attended by millions of his supporters, activists and admirers. At his funeral, more than 10,00,000 of his followers were initiated into Buddhism by Bhadant Anand Kaushalyan, as Ambedkar had organized a Buddhist conversion ceremony in Mumbai on 16 December 1956. After his death, Ambedkar was survived by his second wife Savita Ambedkar, who was the first person to convert to Buddhism after Ambedkar (along with Ambedkar) in the Dalit Buddhist movement. His wife's name before marriage was Dr. Sharda Kabir. Dr. Savita Ambedkar died as a Buddhist on 29 May 2003 at the age of 94. And son Yashwant Ambedkar Ambedkar's grandson, Prakash Ambedkar, leads the Bharipa Bahujan Mahasangh and has been a member of both houses of the Indian Parliament.

A memorial has been erected at Ambedkar's residence at 26 Alipur Road in Delhi. Ambedkar Jayanti is a public holiday. In 1990, he was posthumously awarded India's highest civilian honour, the Bharat Ratna. Every year, more than two million people gather at Chaityabhoomi (Mumbai), Deekshabhoomi (Nagpur) and Bhim Janmabhoomi (Mhow) on his birth anniversary (14 April), Mahaparinirvana (death anniversary) (6 December) and Dhammachakra Pravartan Divas (14 October) to pay their tributes to him. Thousands of bookstores have been set up here, and books are sold. Ambedkar's message to his followers was - "Be educated, be organised, struggle". Ambedkarism is the ideology and philosophy of Ambedkar. The subjects of freedom, equality, brotherhood, Buddhism, scientificism, humanism, truth, non-violence etc. are the principles of Ambedkarism. The main objectives include the elimination of untouchability, social reform among Dalits, propagation and promotion of Buddhism in India, protection of rights and fundamental rights contained in the Indian Constitution, creation of a moral and caste-free society and progress of India. Ambedkarism is a social, political and religious ideology.

Bhimrao Ambedkar was a talented and militant writer. 32 books and monographs (22 complete and 10 incomplete books), 10 memoranda, evidence and statements, 10 research documents, reviews of articles and books and 10 prefaces and predictions are his many compositions in the English language. He had knowledge of 13 languages, including Marathi (mother tongue), English, Hindi, Pali, Sanskrit, Gujarati, German, Persian, French, Kannada and Bengali are the languages included in this. Ambedkar has written more than any other politician of his time. Most of his writings are in English. Always active and engaged in social struggle, he has written a large collection of books, essays, articles and speeches. He was a man of unusual talent. His literary works are known for their unique social outlook and scholarship, which reflect his farsightedness and thinking ahead of his time. Ambedkar's texts are widely read in India and all over the world. His book 'Bhagwan Buddha and His Dhamma' is the 'scripture of Indian Buddhists' and is important in Buddhist countries. His D.Sc. thesis The Problem of the Rupee: Its Origin and Its Solution led to the establishment of the central bank of India, i.e. Reserve Bank of India.

The Education Department of the Maharashtra Government has planned to publish the entire literature of Babasaheb Ambedkar in several volumes. Under this, a new edition of the book is being published. Till date, 22 volumes have been published in English language under the name 'Dr. Babasaheb Ambedkar: Writings and Speeches' and their number of pages is more than 15 thousand. The first volume of this huge project was published on Ambedkar's birthday, 14 April 1979. Considering the importance and popularity of the volumes of 'Dr. Babasaheb Ambedkar: Writings and Speeches', Dr. Ambedkar Pratishthan of the Ministry of Social Justice and Empowerment of the Government of India planned to publish Hindi translations of these volumes and under this plan, till date 21 volumes have been published in Hindi language under the name "Baba Saheb Dr. Ambedkar: Complete Works". Many editions of these Hindi volumes have been published.

Ambedkar was a successful journalist and an effective editor. He believed that newspapers would bring progress in society. He considered newspapers to be very important in the movement. He published and edited several newspapers and five magazines to bring awareness in the exploited and Dalit society. These helped significantly in taking his Dalit movement forward. [He said, "To make any movement successful, newspapers are required. If there is no newspaper for the movement, then the condition of that movement is like a bird with broken wings." Dr. Ambedkar is the pillar of Dalit journalism because he is the first editor, founder and publisher of Dalit journalism. Dr. Ambedkar published all the newspapers in Marathi language because his working area was Maharashtra and Marathi is the common language there. And at that time the exploited and Dalit people of Maharashtra were not very educated, they could only understand Marathi. For several decades, he edited five Marathi magazines, which include Mooknayak (1920), Janata (1930), Bahishkrit Bharat (1927), Samta (1928) and Prabuddha Bharat (1956). In these five newspapers, Babasaheb Ambedkar expressed his views on the country's social, political and economic issues. In 1987, writer and thinker Gangadhar Pantawane wrote a thesis for PhD on Ambedkar's journalism for the first time in India. In it, Pantawane has written about Ambedkar that, "This Mook Nayak brought the people of the outcast India to the enlightened India. Babasaheb was a great journalist.

On 31 January 1920, Babasaheb started his first Marathi fortnightly paper named "Mook Nayak" to expose the atrocities on the untouchables. Its editors were Ambedkar and Panduram Nandram Bhatkar. The top parts of this paper had the words of Saint Tukaram. For this, financial aid of Rs 25,000 was also received from Chhatrapati Shahu Maharaj of Kolhapur Institute. 'Mook Nayak' was the voice of the mute Dalits in every way, in which their sufferings spoke. This paper instilled a new consciousness among the Dalits and provoked them to agitate for their rights. Ambedkar went to England for studies and this paper was closed in 1923 due to financial constraints, but he continued to spread a wave of consciousness. He was successful in his objective.

After the closure of Mooknayak, Ambedkar soon launched another Marathi fortnightly "Bahishkrit Bharat" on 3 April 1924. It was edited by Dr. Ambedkar himself. This paper was published from Bombay. Through this, he used to bring forward the problems and complaints of the untouchable society and also used to answer his critics. In an editorial of this paper, he wrote that if Bal Gangadhar Tilak had been born among the untouchables, he would not have raised the slogan "Swaraj is my birthright" but he would have said "Eradication of untouchability is my birthright." This paper also did an important work of Dalit awakening. The top parts of this newspaper had the words of Saint Dnyaneshwar. A total of 34 issues of this fortnightly were published. Due to financial difficulties, it was closed in November 1929.

10. Vallabhbhai Patel

Birth on 31 October, 1875

Death on 15 December, 1950

Poem on Sardar Vallabhbhai Patel

Such an image of the Iron Man

Never seen or imagined

There was a roar of a lion in his voice

There was a call of tenderness in his heart

The form of unity that he created

Changed the map of the country in a moment

He was the leader of the poor

He was iron for the enemies

He kept flowing like a storm

He kept blazing like a volcano

Becoming Gandhi's weapon of non-violence

He kept smelling in the world like a Brahmastra

The corridors of history search for him

Such a Sardar Patel is not found in the whole world now

Introduction

Sardar Vallabhbhai Patel was a freedom fighter of India. After India's independence, he became the first Home Minister and Deputy Prime Minister. Patel, who was leading the Bardoli Satyagraha, was given the title of Sardar by the women there on the success of the Satyagraha. Patel is also called the Bismarck of India and the Iron Man for playing a central role in the geopolitical integration of India, which was scattered in various princely states after independence.

Biography

Patel was born in a (Gujjar) farmer family in Nadiad, Gujarat. He was the fourth child of Jhaverbhai Patel and Ladba Devi. Somabhai, Narsibhai and Vitthalbhai were his elders. His education was mainly through self-study. He went to London and studied to be a barrister and after returning started practicing law in Ahmedabad. Inspired by the ideas of Mahatma Gandhi, he participated in the freedom movement of India.

Kheda struggle

Sardar Patel's first and biggest contribution in the freedom movement was in the Kheda struggle. Kheda division of Gujarat was in the grip of severe drought in those days. The farmers demanded relief from heavy taxes from the British government. When this was not accepted, Sardar Patel, Gandhiji and others led the farmers and motivated them not to pay taxes. Finally the government bowed down and relief was given in taxes that year. This was Sardar Patel's first success.

Bardoli Satyagraha

Bardoli Satyagraha was a major farmer movement that took place in Gujarat in the year 1928 during the Indian freedom struggle, which was led by Vallabhbhai Patel. At that time the provincial government had increased the rent of the farmers by thirty percent. Patel strongly opposed this rent increase. The government took strict measures to crush this satyagraha movement, but ultimately it was forced to accept the demands of the farmers. A judicial officer Bloomfield and a revenue officer Maxwell investigated the entire matter and declared the 22 percent rent increase wrong and reduced it to 6.03 percent. After the success of this satyagraha movement, the women there gave the title of 'Sardar' to Vallabhbhai Patel. Explaining the relationship between the peasant struggle and the national freedom struggle in the context of the Bardoli peasant struggle, Gandhiji said that every such struggle, every effort is taking us closer to Swaraj and these struggles can prove to be more helpful than the direct struggle for Swaraj in taking us all to the destination of Swaraj.

After Independence

Although most of the provincial Congress committees were in favour of Patel, respecting Gandhiji's wish, Patel ji kept himself away from the race for the post of Prime Minister and supported Nehru for this. He was given the work of Deputy Prime Minister and Home Minister. But even after this, the relations between Nehru and Patel remained tense. Due to this, on many occasions both of them had threatened to resign from their posts. As Home Minister, his first priority was to integrate the princely states into India. He accomplished this without shedding any blood. He had to send the army only for Operation Polo of Hyderabad State. He is known as the Iron Man of India for his great contribution in the unification of India. He died in 1950. After this, Nehru had very little opposition left within the Congress.

Integration of Native States (Princely States)

Sardar Patel, along with VP Menon, had started working to merge many native states with India just before independence (during the transition period). Patel and Menon explained to the native kings that it would not be possible to give them autonomy. As a result, except for three, all the other princely states willingly accepted the proposal of merging with India. Only the kings of Jammu and Kashmir, Junagadh and Hyderabad State did not agree to do so. When there was a lot of opposition against the Nawab of Junagadh, he fled to Pakistan and Junagadh also merged with India. When the Nizam of Hyderabad rejected the proposal of merging with India, Sardar Patel sent the army there and made the Nizam surrender. But Nehru kept Kashmir with himself saying that this problem is an international problem.

Writing work and published books

Sardar Patel, who lived a life of constant struggle, did not get the opportunity to write books independently, but a vast literature is available in the form of his letters, comments and lectures, which have been compiled and published in various forms. The most important among these are Sardar Patel's letters, which have the importance of documents in the context of the freedom struggle. These letters from the period 1945 to 1950 AD were first published in 10 volumes (in English) by Navjeevan Prakashan Mandir under the editorship of Durga Das. Selected correspondence from this vast collection was also published in two volumes under the editorship of V. Shankar, whose Hindi translation was also published. These compilations not only contain Sardar Patel's letters but also important letters written to him by other persons in those contexts. Many books have also been prepared by compiling his literature written in various forms, focusing on various subjects. The details of his entire available literature are as follows:-

Sardar Patel: Selected Correspondence (1945-1950) - In two volumes, Editor- V. Shankar, First Edition-1976, [Navjeevan Prakashan Mandir, Ahmedabad]

Special and Unique Letters of Sardar Shri (1918-1950) - In two volumes, Editor- Ganesh Ma. Nandurkar, First Edition-1981 [Distributor- Navjeevan Prakashan Mandir, Ahmedabad]
Partition of India (Prabhat Prakashan, New Delhi)
Gandhi, Nehru, Subhash
Economic and Foreign Policy
Muslims and Refugees
Kashmir and Hyderabad

11. A. P. J. Abdul Kalam

Birth on 15 October 1931

Death on 27 July 2015

Precious and inspiring words

To reach heights, power i.e. ability is required, whether that height is of Everest or your career.

English is very important. At present, the basic knowledge of science is present only in English. But I believe that after a few decades, our language will also have the basic knowledge of science and at that time we will also be able to make changes like the Japanese.

A good book is equal to a hundred friends, but a good friend is equal to the whole library. Therefore, it is better to have a good friend.

Man needs difficulties in life, because these difficulties make us experience the joy of success.

We should not lose hope nor should we allow ourselves to lose.

A. P. J. Abdul Kalam, popularly known as the Missile Man and the People's President, was the eleventh elected President of the Republic of India. He was a former President of India, renowned scientist and engineer. He worked primarily as a scientist and science administrator for four decades in the Defence Research and Development Organisation (DRDO) and the Indian Space Research Organisation (ISRO) and was also involved in India's civilian space programme and military missile development efforts. He came to be known as the Missile Man of India for his work in the development of ballistic missile and launch vehicle technology. He played a pivotal, organisational, technical and political role in India's Pokhran-II nuclear tests in 1998, the second time since India's first original nuclear test in 1974. Kalam was elected President of India in 2002 with the support of both the ruling Bharatiya Janata Party and the opposition Indian National Congress. After serving a five-year term, he returned to his civilian life of education, writing and public service. He received many prestigious awards including the Bharat Ratna, India's highest civilian honour.

Early life

He was born on 15 October 1931 in a middle class Muslim family in Dhanushkodi village (Rameswaram, Tamil Nadu). His father Jainulabdeen was neither well educated nor wealthy. His father used to rent boats to fishermen. Abdul Kalam lived in a joint family. The size of the family can be estimated from the fact that he himself was a brother and sister and three families used to live in the house. His father had a great influence on Abdul Kalam's life. He may not have been educated, but his dedication and the values he had given him were very useful for Abdul Kalam. At the age of five, he was initiated into the Panchayat Primary School of Rameswaram. His teacher Iyadurai Solomon had told him that to achieve success and favorable results in life, one must understand and master the three powers of intense desire, faith and expectation.

Abdul Kalam also worked as a newspaper distributor to continue his primary education. Kalam received his bachelor's degree in space science from Madras Institute of Technology in 1950. After graduation, he joined the Indian Defense Research and Development Institute to work on the hovercraft project. In 1962, he joined the Indian Space Research Organization where he successfully played his role in many satellite launch projects. As project director, he played an important role in the construction of India's first indigenous satellite launch vehicle SLV 3, which successfully launched the Rohini satellite into space in July 1982.

Scientific life

In 1962, he joined the Indian Space Research Organization. As Project Director, Abdul Kalam got the credit for making India's first indigenous satellite (SLV III) missile. In 1980, he placed the Rohini satellite near the Earth's orbit. Thus, India also became a member of the International Space Club. He is also credited with promoting the ISRO Launch Vehicle Program. Kalam designed indigenous target piercing guided missiles. He made missiles like Agni and Prithvi with indigenous technology. Kalam was the Science Advisor to the Defense Minister and Secretary of the Department of Defense Research and Development from July 1992 to December 1999. He used strategic missile systems as firearms. Similarly, the second nuclear test in Pokhran was also done by mixing it with nuclear energy. In this way, India achieved success in acquiring the capability to manufacture nuclear weapons. Kalam gave a unique vision to make India's development level state-of-the-art in the field of science by 2020. He was also the Chief Scientific Advisor to the Government of India. In 1982, he returned to the Indian Defense Research and Development Institute as Director and focused all his attention on the development of "Guided Missile". Much of the credit for the successful testing of Agni Missile and Prithvi Missile goes to him. In July 1992, he was appointed Scientific Advisor in the Indian Defense Ministry. Under his supervision, India conducted its second successful nuclear test in Pokhran in 1998 and joined the list of nuclear-powered nations.

He was elected President. He was made the candidate of the NDA constituent parties supported by the Bharatiya Janata Party, which was supported by all parties except the left parties. On 18 July 2002, Kalam was elected President of India by a ninety percent majority and he was sworn in as President in the Ashoka Chamber of the Parliament House on 25 July 2002. Prime Minister Atal Bihari Vajpayee, members of his cabinet and officials were present in this brief ceremony. His tenure ended on 25 July 2007. Abdul Kalam was very disciplined in his personal life. He was a vegetarian. He has written his biography Wings of Fire in a style that provides guidance to Indian youth. His second book 'Guiding Souls - Dialogues of the Purpose of Life' reveals spiritual thoughts. He has also written poems in Tamil language. It is also known that his books are in great demand in South Korea and they are liked very much there. Although Abdul Kalam was not a person from the political field, due to his nationalist thinking and welfare policies of India after becoming the President, he can be considered politically successful to some extent. He has clarified his vision in his book India 2020. He wanted to see India become the world leader in the field of space science and for this he also had an action plan. He kept thinking of making India a super power in the field of nuclear weapons. He wanted technological development in other fields of science as well. Kalam said that the field of 'software' should be free from all taboos so that more and more people can benefit from its utility. In such a situation, information technology will be able to develop at a rapid pace. However, his views on peace and weapons are controversial.

After leaving presidential duties

After leaving office, Kalam became an Honorary Fellow and a Visiting Professor at the Indian Institute of Management Shillong, Indian Institute of Management Ahmedabad, Indian Institute of Management Indore and Indian Institute of Science, Bangalore. He became Chancellor of the Indian Institute of Space Science and Technology, Thiruvananthapuram, Professor of Aerospace Engineering at Anna University and adjunct at several other academic and research institutions across India. He taught information technology at Banaras Hindu University and Anna University, and information technology at the International Institute of Information Technology, Hyderabad. In May 2012, Kalam launched the "What Can I Give Movement", a program for the youth of India, with a central theme of defeating corruption. He also enjoyed writing Tamil poetry and playing the South Indian string instrument called the Vennai.

Kalam listened to Carnatic devotional music every day and believed in Hindu culture. He was nominated for the "MTV Youth Icon of the Year" in 2003 and 2006. In the 2011 Hindi film I Am Kalam, Kalam's positive influence on a poor but bright child was portrayed. The child, Chhotu, a Rajasthani boy, renames himself Kalam in his honour. In 2011, Kalam was criticised by civil groups over his stand on the Koodankulam Nuclear Power Plant. He supported the setting up of the power plant. He was accused of not talking to the local people. He is known to be a capable nuclear scientist, but protesters were hostile towards him, unhappy with the assurances he provided about the plant's safety features.

Death

On the evening of 27 July 2015, Abdul Kalam was giving a lecture on 'habitable planet' at Indian Institute of Management Shillong when he suffered a massive cardiac arrest and collapsed. At around 6:30 pm, he was taken to the ICU at Bethany Hospital in critical condition and his death was confirmed after two hours. Hospital CEO John Silo said that when Kalam was brought to the hospital, his pulse and blood pressure had dropped. About 9 hours before his death, he had tweeted that he was going to Shillong IIM for a lecture. Kalam was going to be 84 years old in October 2015. Meghalaya Governor V. Shanmukhanathan; on hearing the news of Abdul Kalam's admission to the hospital, reached the hospital directly. Later, Shanmukhanathan said that despite the efforts of the medical team to save Kalam, he died at 7:45 pm.

Funeral

Immediately after his death, Kalam's body was brought from Shillong to Guwahati by an Indian Air Force helicopter. From where, the next day on 28 July, the body of former President APJ Abdul Kalam was brought to Delhi on Tuesday afternoon by an Air Force aircraft C-130 J Hercules. The plane landed at Palam Airport at around 12:15. The security forces brought Kalam's body down from the plane with full state honors. There, Prime Minister Narendra Modi, President Pranab Mukherjee, Delhi Chief Minister Arvind Kejriwal and the chiefs of the three armies welcomed it and offered wreaths on Kalam's body. After this, Kalam's body wrapped in the tricolor was taken to his residence 10 Rajaji Marg in a gun carriage with full respect. Here many dignitaries including former Prime Minister Manmohan Singh, Congress President Sonia Gandhi, Rahul Gandhi and Uttar Pradesh Chief Minister Akhilesh Yadav paid tribute to him. The Government of India announced a seven-day state mourning as a mark of respect to the former President on his demise.

12. Bal Gangadhar Tilak

(Born on 23 July 1856 Died on 1 August 1920)

Born Keshav Gangadhar Tilak, he was an Indian nationalist, teacher, social reformer, lawyer and a freedom fighter. He was the first popular leader of the Indian freedom struggle; the British colonial authorities called him "Father of Indian unrest". He also received the honorific title of "Lokmanya", which means accepted by the people (as their leader). He is also called the father of Hindu nationalism. Tilak was one of the first and strongest advocates of Swaraj during the British Raj, and was a strong radical in the Indian conscience. His Marathi slogan "Swarajya ha majha janmasiddha haq ahe aani to mi milvaanaarcha" (Swaraj is my birthright and I will have it) became very famous. He formed a close alliance with many leaders of the Indian National Congress, including Bipin Chandra Pal, Lala Lajpat Rai, Aurobindo Ghosh, V.O. Chidambaram Pillai and Muhammad Ali Jinnah.

Early life

Tilak was born on 23 July 1856 in Chikhli, a village in Ratnagiri district of present-day Maharashtra in British India. He was among the first generation of Indians to receive modern college education. He taught mathematics in schools and colleges for some time. He was a strong critic of English education and believed that it taught disrespect for Indian civilization. He founded the Deccan Education Society to improve the standard of education in India.

Political journey

Tilak started two daily newspapers, Memratha Darpan in English and Kesari in Marathi, which became very popular among the people. Tilak strongly criticized the cruelty of the British rule and the inferiority complex towards Indian culture. He demanded that the British government immediately grant complete independence to the Indians. He was sent to jail several times for his articles published in Kesari. Tilak joined the Indian National Congress but soon he started speaking against the moderate attitude of the Congress. In 1907, the Congress split into the extremist group and the moderate group. Lala Lajpat Rai and Bipin Chandra Pal were included in the extremist group along with Tilak. These three came to be known as Lal-Bal-Pal. In 1908, Tilak supported the bomb attack of revolutionaries Prafulla Chaki and Khudiram Bose, due to which he was sent to Mandalay jail in Burma (now Myanmar). After being released from jail, he again joined the Congress and in 1916 founded the All India Home Rule League with Annie Besant and Muhammad Ali Jinnah.

Indian National Congress

Tilak joined the Indian National Congress in 1890. However, he was opposed to its moderate attitude, especially its fight for independence. He was one of the most prominent radicals of his time. Despite being personally opposed to early marriage, Tilak was opposed to the 1891 Age of Consent Bill, which he saw as an interference in Hindu religion and a dangerous precedent. The Act raised the minimum age for a girl to get married from 10 to 12 years.

Social contributions and legacy

Tilak started two daily newspapers, Kesari in Marathi and Maratha in English, which became very popular among the masses. Tilak was highly critical of the cruelty of British rule and its inferiority complex towards Indian culture. He demanded that the British government immediately grant Poorna Swaraj to Indians. He was imprisoned several times for his articles published in Kesari. Tilak joined the Indian National Congress but soon he started speaking against the moderate attitude of the Congress. In 1907, the Congress split into the Extremist Group and the Moderate Group. The Extremist Group included Tilak along with Lala Lajpat Rai and Bipin Chandra Pal. These three came to be known as Lal-Bal-Pal. In 1908, Tilak supported the bomb attack of revolutionaries Prafulla Chaki and Khudiram Bose, due to which he was sent to Mandalay jail in Burma (now Myanmar). After being released from jail, he again joined the Congress and in 1916 founded the All India Home Rule League with Annie Besant and Muhammad Ali Jinnah.

Death

By the time Tilak returned home to attend the Amritsar meeting of the Congress in 1919, he had softened to the extent that he did not oppose Gandhi's policy of boycotting the elections to the Legislative Council established through the Montagu-Chelmsford reforms. Instead, Tilak advised the delegates to follow a policy of responsive cooperation in implementing reforms that introduced some level of Indian participation in regional governments. But before he could give a decisive direction to the new reforms, he died in Bombay on 1 August 1920. Paying posthumous tribute to him, Gandhiji called him the maker of modern India and Jawaharlal Nehru called him the father of the Indian Revolution. "Swaraj is my birth right" I am the only one. Tilak died on 1 August 1920 in Mumbai.

Tilak wrote many books but his best work is Geeta Rahasya written in Mandalay jail on the interpretation of Shrimad Bhagavad Gita and it has been translated in many languages.

The details of all the books written by him are as follows

Vedic period determination
Aryans' original place of residence
Shrimad Bhagavad Gita Rahasya or Karmayoga Shastra
Vedic period determination and Vedanga Jyotish
Hindutva
Tilak's letters to Shyamji Krishna Verma
All his books were first published in Marathi, English and Hindi from Lokmanya Tilak Mandir, Narayan Paith, Pune. Later they were published by other publishers as well.

13. Mangal Pandey

(Birth on 19 July 1827, Death on 8 April 1857)

Mangal Pandey was an Indian freedom fighter who played an important role in India's first war of independence in 1857. He was a soldier of the 34th Bengal Infantry of the East India Company. The then British rule declared him a rebel, while the common Hindustani respects him as a hero of the freedom struggle. A postage stamp was issued in his honor by the Government of India in 1984 for his important role in India's freedom struggle.

Mangal Pandey was born in a Brahmin family on 19 July 1827 in a village named Nagwa in Ballia district of Uttar Pradesh in India. However, some historians consider his birthplace to be Surhurpur village in Faizabad. His father's name was Diwakar Pandey. Mangal Pandey joined the army of the British East India Company in 1849 at the age of 22.

Revolt of 1857

The rebellion started because of a gun. The soldiers were given Pattern 1853 Enfield guns which were of 0.577 caliber and were more powerful and accurate than the old Brown Bess which was in use for many decades. The new gun used a modern system of firing bullets (percussion cap) but the process of loading bullets in the gun was old. To load the new Enfield gun, the cartridge had to be opened by biting it with the teeth and the gunpowder filled in it had to be filled in the barrel of the gun and then the cartridge had to be inserted. The outer cover of the cartridge had fat which protected it from water dampness. A rumour had spread among the soldiers that the fat used in the cartridges was made from pig and cow meat.

On 29 March 1857, Mangal Pandey, who was a resident of Dugwa Rahimpur (Faizabad), attacked and injured the regiment officer Lieutenant Bagh near the Barrackpore Parade Ground, Calcutta. According to General John Hearsey, Mangal Pandey was in some kind of religious madness. The General ordered Jamadar Ishwari Prasad to arrest Mangal Pandey, but the Jamadar refused. Except for one soldier, Sheikh Paltu, the entire regiment refused to arrest Mangal Pandey. Mangal Pandey openly asked his comrades to revolt, but when no one listened, he tried to take his own life with his gun. But he was only injured in this attempt. Mangal Pandey was court-martialed on 6 April 1857 and hanged on 8 April.

Result of the revolt

This spark of revolt ignited by Mangal Pandey did not die out. A month later, on 10 May 1857, there was a revolt in Meerut cantonment. This revolt spread all over northern India in no time, which gave a clear message to the British that ruling India was not as easy as they thought. Only after this, 34 thousand 735 English laws were implemented on the people of Hindustan so that no soldier like Mangal Pandey could rebel against the Indian rulers again.

14. Khudiram Bose

(Birth on 3 December, 1889, Death on 11 August, 1908)

Khudiram Bose was born on 3 December, 1889 in Habibpur village of Midnapore district in Bengal to Trailokya Nath Bose. Khudiram Bose's parents died when he was very young. His elder sister raised him. After the partition of Bengal in 1905, Khudiram Bose jumped into the country's liberation movement. Khudiram Bose started his revolutionary life under the leadership of Satyen Bose. He was a revolutionary who was hanged for the freedom of India at the age of just 19. The history of the Indian freedom struggle is filled with hundreds of heroic exploits of revolutionaries. One name in the list of such revolutionaries is that of Khudiram Bose.

Against British Imperialism

Khudiram Bose started participating in political activities from his school days. In those days, even small Indian school children used to hate the British. They used to participate in rallies and rallies and raise slogans against British imperialism. Bose was so passionate about freeing Mother India from the shackles of slavery that he left his studies after the ninth grade and jumped into the war of independence with a shroud tied on his head.

Party member

He became a member of the Revolutionary Party and played an important role in distributing Vande Mataram pamphlets. He also participated enthusiastically in the movement against the partition of Bengal in 1905.

Participation in the Boycott Movement

The police caught Bose on 28 February 1906 while he was distributing a pamphlet called Sonar Bangla. But Bose was strong. Bose beat up the police and managed to escape from their clutches. On 16 May 1906, the police once again arrested him, but he was released with a warning due to his young age. Bose was also involved in the bomb blast incident at Narayangarh railway station in Bengal on 6 December 1907. He actively participated in the movement to boycott English goods.

Muzaffarpur incident

In those days, Kolkata's Chief Presidency Magistrate Kingsford was very notorious for humiliating and punishing political workers. The revolutionaries assigned the task of eliminating him to Prafulla Chaki and Khudiram Bose. Sensing the anger of the people against Kingsford, the government sent him to Muzaffarpur as a session judge for his safety. But both the revolutionaries also followed him. After studying Kingsford's activities, they threw a bomb on Kingsford's carriage as soon as he came out of the European Club on 30 April 1908. But unfortunately two European women, the wife and daughter of an advocate named Pingle Kennedy, were sitting in a carriage of similar size and shape and they were killed. The revolutionaries fled from the scene thinking that they had succeeded in killing Kingsford.

Against the British Raj

In the initial phase of the Indian freedom movement, there were many revolutionaries who raised their voice against the British Raj. Khudiram Bose was probably the youngest revolutionary in the history of India's freedom struggle, who can be called the son of Mother India. Saddened by the partition of Bengal, Khudiram Bose lit a torch in the freedom struggle with his revolutionary activities. He planted a bomb on the vehicle of a British officer to spread fear among the British Raj.

Conspiracy by the revolutionaries

In those days, Kingsford was the Chief Presidency Magistrate in Calcutta. He was a very strict and cruel officer. That officer used to harass the patriots, especially the revolutionaries a lot. He used to torture them in many ways. The revolutionaries had decided to kill him. Virendra Kumar Ghosh, the leader of the Yugantar Revolutionary Party, announced that Kingsford would be killed in Muzaffarpur itself. Khudiram Bose and Prapulla Chaki were chosen for this task. Both these revolutionaries were very intelligent. There was no limit to their happiness. They were entrusted with the task of killing those who harassed the patriots. One day both of them reached Muzaffarpur. They stayed in a Dharamshala there for eight days. During this time they kept a close watch on Kingsford's daily routine and activities. There was a club near his bungalow. British officers and their families often went there in the evening.

On the evening of April 30, 1908, Kingsford and his wife reached the club. At 8:30 in the night, Mrs. Kennedy and her daughter were coming home from the club in their carriage. Their carriage was red in colour and it was exactly similar to Kingsford's carriage. Khudiram Bose and his companion threw a bomb on it thinking it to be Kingsford's carriage. The carriage was blown to pieces in no time. Both the mother and daughter riding in it died. The revolutionaries fled with the belief that they had succeeded in killing Kingsford.

Arrest of Khudiram Bose

Khudiram Bose and Ghosh reached a railway station after running for 25 miles. The police suspected Khudiram Bose of this bomb blast and the British police started chasing him and surrounded him at Vani railway station. Seeing himself surrounded by the police, Prafulla Chand shot himself and attained martyrdom but Khudiram was caught. There was no feeling of fear in his mind. Khudiram Bose was put in jail and a murder case was filed against him. In his statement, he admitted that he had tried to kill Kingsford. But he regretted that innocent Kennedy and his daughter were killed by mistake.

Death sentence

The trial lasted only five days. He was presented in the court on June 8, 1908 and on June 13 he was sentenced to death. Such a serious case and it ended in just five days. This will remain a joke in the history of justice. On 11 August 1908, this brave revolutionary was hanged. He sacrificed his life for the freedom of the country.

Popularity

The magistrate who had ordered his hanging in Muzaffarpur jail later said that Khudiram Bose had walked towards the gallows fearlessly like a lion cub. When Khudiram was martyred, he was 19 years old. After his martyrdom, Khudiram became so popular that the weavers of Bengal started weaving a special type of dhoti in his name. His martyrdom had created a wave of patriotism in the entire country. Songs were composed to immortalize his courageous contribution and his sacrifice was expressed in the form of folk songs. Emotional songs were composed in his honor which are sung by the folk singers of Bengal even today.

15. Lal Bahadur Shastri

(Birth on 2 October 1904, Death on 11 January 1966)

Lal Bahadur Shastri Biography and History

Shastri ji was the second Prime Minister of India. Due to Nehru ji's death during his tenure, Shastri ji was nominated to this post on 9 June 1964. His position was second, but his rule was 'unique'. This simple and calm person was awarded the country's highest honor 'Bharat Ratna' in 1966. Shastri ji was a great freedom fighter, he followed the footsteps of Mahatma Gandhi and Jawahar Lal Nehru. He kept the country under control during the India-Pakistan war of 1965, and gave the right direction to the army.

Shastri ji was born on 2 October 1904 in Mughalsarai (Uttar Pradesh) British India. His father's name was Munshi Sharda Prasad Srivastava, he was a primary school teacher and was addressed as 'Munshi ji'. His mother's name was Ram Dulari. In childhood, Lal Bahadur ji was called 'Nanhe' by family members. Shastri's father died in his childhood. After this, Lal Bahadur ji's mother brought him to her father Hazari Lal's house in Mirzapur. After some time, his maternal grandfather also died.

His primary education was done in Mirzapur and further studies were done in Harishchandra High School and Kashi Vidyapeeth. Lal Bahadur ji graduated in Sanskrit language. He received the title of 'Shastri' from Kashi Vidyapeeth. From this time onwards, he added 'Shastri' to his name. After this, he started being known as Shastri. In 1928, he married Lalita Shastri. They had six children. One of his sons Anil Shastri was a member of the Congress Party.

Lal Bahadur Shastri, a young Satyagrahi

In the freedom struggle, Shastriji gave the slogan 'Maro Nahi Maro', which intensified the flame of freedom in the whole country. In 1920, Shastriji jumped into the freedom struggle and joined the 'Bharat Sevak Sangh'. He was a 'Gandhian' leader, who devoted his entire life to the service of the country and the poor. Shastriji used to participate in all movements and programs, as a result of which he had to go to jail many times. He actively participated in the 'Non-Cooperation Movement' in 1921, 'Dandi March' in 1930, and the Quit India Movement in 1942.

The freedom struggle in India was also intensified during the Second World War. Netaji Subhash Chandra Bose formed the 'Azad Hind Fauj' and gave it the slogan of "Dilli Chalo" and at the same time, on 8 August 1942, Gandhiji's 'Quit India Movement' gained momentum. During this time, Shastriji gave the slogan of "Do or Die" to awaken the Indians, but on 9 August 1942, Shastriji changed this slogan in Allahabad and appealed to the countrymen by making it "Maro Nahi Maro". During this movement, Shastriji remained underground for eleven days, then he was arrested on 19 August 1942.

Lal Bahadur Shastri, Leader of Independent India

In independent India, he was appointed Secretary of the Parliament of Uttar Pradesh. Under the shadow of Govind Vallabh Pant's cabinet, he was given the responsibility of police and transport. During this time, Shastriji appointed the first woman conductor and in the police department, he made a rule to control the crowd by spraying water instead of lathi. In 1951, Shastri Ji was made the General Secretary of the All India National Congress. Lal Bahadur Shastri was always dedicated to the party. He worked hard for the party in the elections of 1952, 1957, 1962 and campaigned for the party and made the Congress win with a huge majority.

Looking at Shastri Ji's ability, he was appointed Prime Minister after the sudden death of Jawaharlal Nehru, but his tenure was very difficult. Capitalist countries and enemy countries made his rule very challenging. Suddenly, in 1965, at 7.30 pm, Pakistan attacked India by air. In this situation, President Sarvepalli Radhakrishnan called a meeting. The heads of the three defense departments and Shastri Ji attended this meeting. During the discussion, the leaders apprised Lal Bahadur Shastri of the entire situation and waited for orders, then Shastri ji replied, "You protect the country and tell me what we have to do?" In this way, during the Indo-Pak war, Shastri ji gave commendable leadership in difficult circumstances and gave the slogan of "Jai Jawan Jai Kisan", which brought unity in the country and India defeated Pakistan, which Pakistan had not imagined, because three years ago China had defeated India in the war.

Lal Bahadur Shastri Death –

Under pressure from Russia and America, Shastri ji met Pakistan President Ayub Khan in Tashkent, the capital of Russia, to sign the peace agreement. It is said that he was pressurised to sign the agreement. He died mysteriously on 11 January 1966, the very night of the agreement. According to that time, Shastri ji had a heart attack, but it is said that his post-mortem was not done because he was poisoned, which was a well-planned conspiracy, which is still a secret buried in the air of Tashkent. In this way, Lal Bahadur Shastri held the command of India for only 18 months. After his death, Gulzari Lal Nanda was again appointed as the acting Prime Minister. His last rites were performed on the banks of river Yamuna and that place was named 'Vijay Ghat'. In 1978, his wife narrated the story of Shastri ji's death in a book named 'Lalita ke Aansoo'. Kuldeep Nayyar, who had gone to Tashkent with Shastri ji, also exposed many facts but no proper results came out. In 2012, his son Sunil Shastri also demanded justice but nothing could be done.

16. Khan Abdul Ghaffar Khan

(Birth on 6 February, 1890, Death on 20 January, 1988)

Khan Abdul Ghaffar Khan was a great politician who participated in the freedom struggle of India and due to his work and dedication, he came to be known as "Sarhadi Gandhi" (Frontier Gandhi), "Bacha Khan" and "Badshah Khan". He was the most prominent and charismatic leader of the Pashtuns (or Pathans; Muslim ethnic group of Pakistan and Afghanistan) in the 20th century, who became a follower of Mahatma Gandhi and came to be known as 'Frontier Gandhi'. Abdul Ghaffar Khan was born in a wealthy family. He has been a person of very firm nature since childhood, so the Afghans started calling him 'Bacha Khan'. He had a great influence on the tribes of the Frontier Province. Being a staunch follower of Gandhi ji, he had the image of 'Frontier Gandhi'. The humble Ghaffar always called himself just a 'soldier of freedom struggle', but his admirers called him 'Badshah Khan'. Gandhi ji also used to address him like this. By participating in national movements, he has suffered severe torture in jails many times. Still, he did not turn away from his original culture. This is the reason why he had a lot of affection towards India.

Khan Abdul Ghaffar Khan was born on 6 February 1890 in Peshawar, then British India, present Pakistan. His great grandfather 'Abdullah Khan' was very truthful and combative. His father 'Bairam Khan' was of calm nature and used to be absorbed in devotion to God. He sent his son Abdul Ghaffar Khan to 'Missionary School' to educate him, the Pathans opposed him a lot. After completing his studies at the missionary school, he came to Aligarh. Social service was his main work during the summer vacations. After completing his education, he started serving the country.

Introduction to Gandhiji

During the 1919 movement against the Rowlatt Act, which allowed the detention of political dissidents without trial, Ghaffar Khan met Gandhiji and entered politics. The following year he joined the Khilafat Movement, which sought a spiritual relationship between Indian Muslims and the Sultan of Turkey, and in 1921 he was elected the district president of the Khilafat Committee in his home state, the North-West Frontier Province.

Establishment of Khudai Khidmatgar

After attending a meeting of the Congress Party in 1929, Ghaffar Khan established Khudai Khidmatgar (Servants of God) and called for the Red Shirt Movement among the Pashtuns. He was first arrested for 3 years on charges of rebellion. After that, he got used to facing torture.

After coming out of jail, he founded an organization named 'Khudai Khidmatgar' to connect the Pathans with the national movement and intensified his movements.

Peace-loving Badshah Khan

When the British imposed martial law in Peshawar in 1919, Abdul Ghaffar Khan proposed peace to the British, but he was arrested.

In 1930, he was again sent to jail for leading a Satyagraha movement and was sent to Gujarat, a part of Punjab at that time. There he met other prisoners from Punjab. He read the scriptures of the Sikh Gurus in the jail and studied the Gita.

Considering the need for Hindu-Muslim unity, he started classes on the Gita and the Quran in the Gujarat jail, where qualified Sanskrit scholars and Maulvis used to run the respective classes. Everyone was influenced by his company and everyone studied all the scriptures like the Gita, the Quran and the Guru Granth Sahib.

Badshah Khan (Khan Abdul Ghaffar Khan) movement supported the non-violent national movement for India's independence and he tried to make the Pashtuns politically aware.
By the late 1930s, Ghaffar Khan became one of Mahatma Gandhi's closest advisors and the Khudai Khidmatgars actively supported the Congress Party until the partition of India in 1947.

His brother Doctor Khan Saheb (1858-1958) was also close to Gandhi and a supporter of the Congress movement.

After the Gandhi-Irwin Pact of 1930, Abdul Ghaffar Khan was released and he started social work.

In the provincial elections of 1937, Congress won a majority in the provincial assembly of the North-West Frontier Province. Khan Saheb was elected the leader of the party and became the Chief Minister. He was arrested in the August Movement of 1942 and was released in 1947.

Ghaffar Khan, who was against the partition of the country, decided to stay in Pakistan, where he continued to fight for the rights of the Pashtun minority and for an autonomous Pashtunistan (or Pathanistan) within Pakistan.

When India was divided, his connection with India was almost broken, but he did not agree with the partition of India in any way. His ideology was completely different from Pakistan. He continued to run the 'Independent Pashtunistan Movement' against Pakistan throughout his life.

He had to pay a heavy price for his principles; he was in jail for many years and after that he had to live in Afghanistan.

He was the main attraction of the 'Congress Centenary Celebration' of 1985. He toured the whole of India in 1970. He returned to Pakistan in 1972.

His memoir "My Life and Struggle" was published in 1969.

17. Lala Lajpat Rai

(Birth on 28 January, 1865, Death on 17 November, 1928)

Lala Lajpat Rai was one of the main revolutionaries who fought against British rule in India. He was known as Punjab Kesari (Lion of Punjab) and was one of the three main leaders of the extremist group of Congress, Lal-Bal-Pal (Lala Lajpat Rai, Bal Gangadhar Tilak and Bipin Chandra Pal). He also founded Punjab National Bank (PNB) and Lakshmi Insurance Company. Lala Lajpat Rai influenced many revolutionaries and one of them was Shaheed Bhagat Singh. In 1928, during the demonstration against the Simon Commission, he was badly injured in the lathi-charge and died on 17 November 1928.

Early life

Lala Lajpat Rai was born on 28 January 1865 in Dudhike village, presently located in Moga district of Punjab. He was the eldest son of Munshi Radha Kishan Azad and Gulab Devi. His father was an Aggarwal of the Bania caste. From childhood, his mother taught him high moral values. Lala Lajpat Rai joined the Government School in Lahore to study law in the year 1889. During college, he came in contact with patriots and future freedom fighters like Lala Hansraj and Pandit Gurudutt. The three became good friends and joined the Arya Samaj founded by Swami Dayanand Saraswati.

Political life

In the year 1885, he passed the law examination in the second division from the Government College and started his law practice in Hisar. Apart from practicing law, Lalaji collected funds for Dayanand College, participated in Arya Samaj functions and Congress activities. He was elected member and secretary of the Hisar Municipality. He moved to Lahore in 1892. Lala Lajpat Rai was one of the three major Hindu nationalist leaders of the Indian National Congress. He was part of the Lal-Bal-Pal trio. Bal Gangadhar Tilak and Bipin Chandra Pal were the other two members of this trio. They formed the Extremist Group to oppose the Moderate Group (earlier led by Gopal Krishna Gokhale) in the Indian National Congress. Lalaji took part in the agitation against the partition of Bengal. He, along with Surendra Nath Banerjee, Bipin Chandra Pal and Aurobindo Ghosh, united the people of Bengal and other parts of the country for a strong campaign for Swadeshi. Lala Lajpat Rai was arrested on 3 May 1907 for creating disturbance in Rawalpindi and was released on 11 November 1907 after being kept in Mandalay Jail for six months.

The freedom struggle had taken a revolutionary turn, so Lalaji wanted to publicize the real situation of India in other countries as well. For this purpose, he went to Britain in 1914. At the same time, the First World War broke out due to which he could not return to India and then went to the United States to get support for India. He founded the Indian Home League of America and wrote a book called "Young India". Through the book, he made serious allegations about the British rule in India and hence it was banned in Britain and India even before it was published. He could return to India only after the World War ended in 1920. After returning, Lala Lajpat Rai led protests and non-cooperation movement in Punjab against the Jallianwala Bagh massacre. During this time he was also arrested several times. He did not agree with Gandhiji's decision to stop the non-cooperation movement due to the Chauri Chaura incident and he founded the Congress Independence Party. Opposition to Simon Commission

In 1928, the British government decided to send the Simon Commission to India to discuss constitutional reforms. There was disappointment and anger among all the people due to the absence of any Indian member in the commission. When the commission came to India in 1929, it was opposed all over India. Lala Lajpat Rai himself led a procession against the Simon Commission. Although the procession was peaceful, the British government brutally lathi-charged the procession. Lala Lajpat Rai suffered serious head injuries and due to which he died on 17 November 1928.

18. Rani Laxmibai

Rani Lakshmibai

Birth

(19 November 1835, Death on18 June 1858)

She was the queen of the Maratha-ruled Jhansi state and a hero of the First Indian War of Independence of 1857. She fought the British Empire's army at the age of just 23 and died on the battlefield.

Lakshmibai was born on 19 November 1835 in a town called Bhadaini in Varanasi (Kashi) district. Her childhood name was Manikarnika but she was fondly called Manu. Her mother's name was Bhagirathibai and father's name was Moropant Tambe. Moropant was a Marathi and was in the service of Maratha Bajirao. Mother Bhagirathibai was a cultured, intelligent and religious woman. Her mother died when she was 18 years old. Since there was no one to take care of Manu at home, the father started taking Manu with him to the court of Peshwa Bajirao II. Where everyone started calling Manu "Lee" lovingly as a playful and beautiful Manu. Manu also received training in weapons along with the study of scriptures in her childhood. In 1842, she was married to the Maratha ruler of Jhansi, King Gangadhar Rao Newalkar and she became the queen of Jhansi. After marriage, she was named Lakshmibai. In 1851, Rani Lakshmibai gave birth to a son. But he died at the age of four months. In 1853, when the health of King Gangadhar Rao deteriorated, he was advised to adopt a son. After adopting a son, King Gangadhar Rao died on 21 November 1853. The adopted son was named Damodar Rao. The British Raj filed a case against the child Damodar Rao in the court under its policy of usurping the state. Although the case was hotly debated, it was dismissed. The British authorities confiscated the state treasury and ordered that her husband's debt be deducted from the queen's annual expenses. As a result, the queen had to leave the Jhansi fort and move to the Rani Mahal in Jhansi. But Rani Lakshmibai did not lose courage and decided to protect the Jhansi state at all costs.

Battle of Jhansi

Jhansi became a major centre of the 1857 war where violence broke out. Rani Lakshmibai started strengthening the security of Jhansi and started forming a volunteer army. Women were recruited in this army and were trained in war. The common people also helped in this war. She gave a prominent place in her army to Jhalkari Bai who was Lakshmibai's lookalike. In the months of September and October 1857, the kings of the neighbouring states of Orchha and Datia attacked Jhansi. The queen successfully thwarted it. In January 1858, the British army started moving towards Jhansi and surrounded the city in the month of March. After two weeks of fighting, the British army captured the city. But Rani managed to escape from the British along with Damodar Rao. Rani fled from Jhansi and reached Kalpi and met Tatya Tope. The combined forces of Tatya Tope and the queen captured a fort in Gwalior with the help of the rebel soldiers of Gwalior. Rani Lakshmibai died fighting the British army at Kota Ki Sarai near Gwalior on 18 June 1858. In his battle report, British General Hughrose commented that Rani Lakshmibai was not only remarkable for her beauty, cleverness and determination, but was also the most dangerous of the rebel leaders.

19. Kasturba Gandhi

(Birth on 11 April, 1869, Death on 22 February, 1944)

If we talk about India's freedom struggle, the names of many women come to our mind, but the woman whose name has become synonymous with freedom is 'Kasturba Gandhi'. Kasturba Gandhi, popularly known as 'Ba', was the wife of the Father of the Nation, Mahatma Gandhi, and she made a significant contribution to India's freedom movement. Despite being illiterate, Kasturba had the wisdom to recognize good and bad. She faced evil boldly throughout her life and on many occasions did not hesitate to warn Gandhiji. According to Mahatma Gandhi, "Among the people who have come in close contact with me and Ba, the majority are those who have many times more respect for Ba than me". She spent her entire life for her husband and country. In this way, Kasturba Gandhi made a valuable contribution to the country's independence and social upliftment.

Early life

Kasturba Gandhi was born on 11 April 1869 in Porbandar city of Kathiawar. Kasturba's father 'Gokuldas Makanji' was an ordinary businessman and Kasturba was his third child. In those days, most people did not educate their daughters and married them at a young age. Kasturba's father was a close friend of Mahatma Gandhi's father and both friends had decided to convert their friendship into a relationship. Kasturba was illiterate in childhood and at the age of only seven, she was engaged to 6-year-old Mohandas and at the young age of thirteen, both of them got married.

Kasturba's early domestic life was very difficult. Her husband Mohandas Karamchand Gandhi was unhappy with her illiteracy and kept taunting her. Mohandas did not like Kasturba dressing up, dressing up and stepping out of the house at all. He tried to control 'Ba' from the very beginning but was not very successful.

Life with Gandhiji

After marriage, the husband and wife lived together till 1888, but after Mohandas migrated to England, she remained alone. In Mohandas' absence, she raised their child Harilal. After completing his education, Gandhi returned from England, but soon he had to go to South Africa. After this, Mohandas came to India in 1896 and took Kasturba with him. From going to South Africa till his death, 'Ba' followed Mahatma Gandhi. She had made her life as simple and ordinary as Gandhi. She always accompanied Gandhi in all his activities. Bapu observed many fasts during the freedom movement and she often remained with him and took care of him during these fasts. She supported Gandhiji very well in South Africa. When she joined the movement there in protest against the condition of Indians, she was arrested and sent to jail with a rigorous sentence of three months. The food served in the jail was inedible, so she decided to eat fruits, but when the officers did not pay heed to her request, she fasted, after which the officers had to bow down.

In 1915, Kasturba also returned to India with Mahatma Gandhi and supported him at every step. Many times when Gandhiji went to jail, she took his place. During the Champaran Satyagraha, she also went there with Gandhiji and told people about the importance of cleanliness, discipline, education etc. During this time, she kept distributing medicines by roaming in the villages. During the Kheda Satyagraha also, Ba kept roaming and encouraging women. After Gandhi's arrest in 1922, she gave a statement like a brave woman and called for abandoning foreign clothes in protest against this arrest. She also visited the villages of Gujarat to spread Gandhiji's message. When Bapu went to jail after Dandi and Dharasana in 1930, Ba took his place and kept boosting the morale of the people. Due to revolutionary activities, she spent most of her time in jail in 1932 and 1933. In 1939, she also participated in Satyagraha against the king of Rajkot state. The ruler of that place, Thakur Saheb, had agreed to give some rights to the people but later he reneged on his promise.

20. Begum Hazrat Mahal

(Birth in 1820 Death, on 7 April 1879)

Begum Hazrat Mahal was the wife of Nawab Wajid Ali Shah of Awadh. In 1857, during India's first war of independence, she revolted against the British East India Company. When the officials of the British East India Company seized the Awadh state and sent her husband Nawab Wajid Ali Shah to Kolkata, Begum Hazrat Mahal took the reins of Awadh in her hands and captured Lucknow. She put her minor son Birjis Qadar on the throne and personally fought the British army. Hazrat Mahal had an unprecedented capacity for organization, due to which the landlords, farmers and soldiers of Awadh province supported her and kept moving forward under her leadership. Although she fought and struggled against the British with all her heart, she ultimately had to face defeat and fled and took refuge in Nepal where she died in 1879.

Early life

Begum Hazrat Mahal was born in 1820 in Faizabad district of Awadh province. Her childhood name was Muhammadi Khatoon. She was a courtesan by profession and when her parents sold her, she came to the royal harem as a Khawasin. After this, she was sold to royal brokers after which she was given the title of Pari and she came to be known as 'Mehak Pari'. When the Nawab of Awadh included her in his royal harem, she became Begum and she got the title of 'Hazrat Mahal' after the birth of her son Birjis Qadr. She was the wife of Tajdar-e-Awadh Nawab Wajid Ali Shah. When the British captured Awadh in 1856 and sent the Nawab to Kolkata, Begum Hazrat Mahal decided to take over the reins of Awadh. She placed her minor son Birjis Qadr on the throne and personally fought the British army.

First War of Independence of 1857

During the First War of Independence of 1857-58, Begum Hazrat Mahal's supporters, led by Raja Jailal Singh, rebelled against the British East India Company's forces and captured Lucknow. After the capture of Lucknow, Hazrat Mahal placed her minor son Birjis Qadr on the throne of Awadh. Subsequently, when the Company's forces recaptured Lucknow and most of Awadh, Begum Hazrat Mahal had to retreat. She then joined Nana Saheb (the Peshwa who led the revolt against the British in Kanpur) and then along with the Maulvi of Faizabad, carried out the Shahjahanpur invasion. She accused the British of interfering in the religion of Hindus and Muslims.

Later life

After being defeated by the British, Begum Hazrat Mahal had to take refuge in Nepal. Initially, Nepal's Rana Prime Minister Jung Bahadur refused but later he was given asylum. After this, he spent his entire life in Nepal where he died in 1879. He was buried in the grounds of Jama Masjid in Kathmandu.

Memorial

The tomb of Begum Hazrat Mahal is located in the middle of Kathmandu near Jama Masjid (at Ghantaghar). This place is not far from Durbar Marg. It is maintained by the Jama Masjid Central Committee. On 15 August 1962, in honor of Begum Hazrat Mahal, the name of 'Old Victoria Park' in Hazratganj, Lucknow was changed to 'Begum Hazrat Mahal Park'. Along with the change of name, a marble memorial was also built here. Festivals like Ramlila, Dussehra and Lucknow Mahotsav are organized in Begum Hazrat Mahal Park. On 10 May 1984, the Government of India issued a postage stamp in her honor.

21. Sarojini Naidu

(Born on 13 February1879, Died on 2 March, 1949)
Saro
On February 13, 1879, Sarojini Naidu was born in Hyderabad. Aghorenath Chattopadhyay, her father, was a Bengali Brahmin who served as the principal of Hyderabad's Nizam's College. She had her education at Cambridge, London, and Madras. After working as a suffragist in England, she became interested in the Indian National Congress's campaign to free India from British domination.

She joined the Indian Nationalist movement and adopted Mahatma Gandhi's philosophy of swaraj. She was detained for taking part in the 1930 Salt March, along with prominent Congress leaders Madan Mohan Malaviya, Jawaharlal Nehru, and Gandhi. One of the key players who spearheaded the Quit India and Civil Disobedience movements was Sarojini. During that period, she was arrested several times by British police, and she even served more than 21 months in jail (1 year, 9 months). She was the first woman to serve as governor of the Dominion of India after being elected president of the Indian National Congress in 1925 and then governor of the United Provinces in 1947.

Naidu's poetry ranges from children's rhymes to more serious works on patriotism, romance, and sorrow. 'In the Bazaars of Hyderabad', published in 1912, is still one of her best-known poems.

She died of a cardiac arrest at Government House in Lucknow on March 2, 1949.